GUATEMALAN WOMEN SPEAK

CIIR is publishing this book to provide a platform from which the voice of Guatemalan women can be heard. Coming out of silence, it has the power to shock. That should not stop us from listening.

First published 1991

Catholic Institute for International Relations,
Unit 3, Canonbury Yard,
190a New North Road, London N1 7BJ

British Library Cataloguing in Publication Data
Hooks, Margaret
    Guatemalan women speak
    I. Title
    972. 81053

    ISBN 1 85287 081 8

Cover and text design by Rich Cowley
All photos by Jenny Matthews

Printed in the UK by Russell Press Ltd, Nottingham

GUATEMALAN WOMEN SPEAK

Margaret Hooks

This book is dedicated to the memory of Alaide Foppa, Guatemalan feminist writer who 'disappeared' in Guatemala City in 1980.

She feels...

Often she feels herself
an abandoned object
forgotten in a dark corner of the house
a piece of fruit eaten from within
by greedy birds,
a shadow without features or matter
a light vibration in still air,
looks pass through her
and she turns to fog
in rude restraining arms.
She would like to be
a juicy orange
clasped by a child
— not rind,
a shining mirror image
— not a transient ghost,
a ringing voice
— not torpid silence,
a voice listened to once in a while.

Alaide Foppa (translation by Jean Franco)

Contents

Acknowledgements   vii
Glossary   viii
Preface   ix

1: EARNING A LIVING
On the finca   2
Lady of the coffee plantation   6
In the market-place   10
'I sell beauty'   14
The picture of health   18
I've given my best years to the United States   24
The union makes us strong   29

2: BEING INDIAN
Making progress   36
A widow's story   40
Away from home   43
Racism   48
Being Indian in Guatemala City   49
Prejudice   53
Defining cultural identity   54
Machismo   58
The attraction of evangelism   59
Exiled from my Quiché home   61
Weavers of the future   67

3: FAMILY AFFAIRS
Marrying for love   76

Catholics and sexuality   77
'The only thing women need men for is martyrdom'   78
Family planning   82
'Children bless a home'   83

4: FIGHTING BACK

Until we find them   86
Fighting in the Guerrilla Army of the Poor   92
Sisterhood is great   96
'Don't talk...'   101
Life as a Carib student leader   102
Option for the poor   106
First woman Labour Minister   110
Censorship   113
Faith in the far-right   114
Revolution and love in the URNG   118
Widows fight for dignity and unity   123

Acknowledgements

It is impossible to acknowledge sufficiently the help and support of the many women in Guatemala who made this book possible. I can never repay their generosity and trust. They have my deepest respect and gratitude, and I regret that the situation in Guatemala is still such that I might be betraying their trust if I were to mention them by name.

My gratitude to Trócaire for providing most of the funding which allowed me to take the time away from journalism to research and write this book. My thanks to Oxfam and War on Want for also providing me with financial assistance. In particular, I would like to mention Patricia Ardón, Deborah Eade, Phil Bloomer and Luis Silva.

I am especially grateful to Sally O'Neill of Trócaire, who not only made the project financially possible but was also a source of encouragement and insight, and to Madge Rondo who initially inspired me to write the book.

Thanks also to Rob Doll, Inmaculada Burke, Karen Bates and George and Irene Tangeman for their kindness and hospitality during my visits to Guatemala and Los Angeles.

A very special thanks to Elsa Vega for transcribing the interviews and for being so enthusiastic about the project, and to Mike Tangeman for his help and support when it looked like this book might never appear.

Glossary

campesino/a   Peasant and/or hired farm labourer.

compañero/a   Term widely used in Latin America to mean friend, husband, wife, lover, colleague, comrade, or simply anyone involved in the same social or political struggle. In this book, it remains untranslated only in the last case.

corte   Long piece of material worn as a skirt.

finca   Plantation or large farm.

huipil   Indian blouse with intricate woven design.

ladino/a   Person of European or part-European descent; also used to describe indigenous people who have adopted *ladino* culture.

quetzal   National unit of currency worth about 12p; also, tropical bird and national emblem of Guatemala.

tortilla   Small, flat corn pancake.

traje   Indian clothing.

Preface

This book is about the lives of Guatemalan women — women who are, on the whole, poor and Indian; women whose voices are seldom heard. Through their stories, we become acquainted with the reality of daily life in their country. But that is not the principal objective of this book. It is, rather, to break with the way in which Guatemalan women are usually presented — as exotic Mayan Indians in a picturesque setting or as the passive victims of a cruel repression — and to allow the women to become, as one of the women interviewed describes it, 'protagonists in our own struggle'.

In these interviews, the women talk about their marriages, their jobs, their families, their religion, their sexuality, culture, racism, machismo and women's liberation: what they want to achieve, their hopes and their dreams. Today, a nascent feminism is beginning to make its presence felt in Guatemala, particularly in the grass roots organisations, trade unions and the national liberation struggle. Some of the women interviewed here talk about what this means for them, about the differences that they believe exist between this and the women's movement in the 'first world' and their need to create 'a new feminism' tailored to the specific conditions in Guatemala.

Parts of Guatemala are still in a state of war, albeit a war forgotten or ignored by many outsiders, and most women's lives have been affected by it. Nearly all of the women in this book have experienced the violence of war firsthand and talk about the effect on their lives. Nevertheless, they do not think of themselves as victims first and foremost. They are women who have taken some form of control over their lives, who have a strong sense of their identity as women, and who have nearly all struggled against passive acceptance of their traditional roles.

The women featured in this book reflect the structure of Guatemalan society. Most of them are poor and indigenous. Five live in exile: two in the United States, two in Mexico and one in another Latin American country. There are also three interviews with women from Guatemala's ruling elite, included to show the thinking of women from sectors responsible for much of their country's social injustice — as has been amply documented elsewhere.

Interviewed in this book are weavers, market women, *campesinas*, teachers, seamstresses, nuns, guerrillas, housewives, domestic servants, lawyers, nurses, students, businesswomen, kitchen assistants, politicians and journalists. All the interviews, except for two, were conducted in Spanish, transcribed and then translated. Because spoken language is different from written language, they were first edited by the author to maintain coherence in what were deliberately unstructured conversations. They were later reworked by the editors to make them more suitable for the present edition. Brief introductions to each interview are provided, containing background information which will help the reader to place the women's stories in the political, social and economic context of Guatemala.

The original idea for this book came about as a result of an interview I carried out in Mexico City in late 1984. A friend recommended that as a journalist covering Guatemala I should interview Juanita, a Guatemalan Indian *campesina* who had fled Guatemala. I decided to obtain her 'testimony', and I prepared myself to meet a timid, unassuming woman, whom I would have to encourage to talk.

In order to put her at her ease, I offered to meet her over lunch in a restaurant. To my surprise, when we sat down at the table Juanita reached into her bag, took out a small tape recorder and placed it on the table. I still had mine discreetly hidden in my pocket, where I had put it so as not to alarm her by recording her words immediately. 'I want to play you some marimba music from my village,' she said, and oblivious to the surprise of the other diners, proceeded to fill the restaurant with this music so loved by Guatemalans.

By this simple act Juanita established some control over our interview, refusing to become the passive recipient of my questions. Our lengthy conversation made me realise that, despite Guatemala's being a key country in the Central American conflict, virtually nothing is known about the daily lives and concerns of Guatemalan women. In our conversation that day, we talked about love and politics, discrimination and religion, Indian customs and political commitment. Juanita's was a story that I knew no newspaper editor would find the space to print, but it was one that I believed should be told.

In 1986 a civilian president was elected in Guatemala for the first time in sixteen years and, although human rights violations continued, a brief period began when people were more willing to talk. The popular organisations were beginning to gather strength and some exiles were making a timorous return. It seemed a good time to undertake interviews for this book, so in November 1986 I began.

Over the next two and a half years I made five lengthy visits to Guatemala. During this time I carried out interviews with more than 40 women, the bulk of which took place in the summer of 1987. Since the majority of the women whom I talked to were poor and Indian, they were also the women most affected by the internal conflict, so some degree of secrecy and much concern for their security surrounded the interviews. Guatemala is a country where for Indians or the poor, talking to a foreigner holding a tape recorder is regarded with suspicion.

The degree to which an interview was successful nearly always depended on being able to form a kind of instant 'friendship' with the women. Empathy had to be quickly established and, most importantly, so had trust. This worked best when the woman herself directed the interview. I had, of course, certain questions that I wanted to ask each one, but nobody was pressed to reply if she didn't want to. All of the women were assured that first names only would be used and that fictitious names could be substituted if they wished; most opted for the latter. Names of villages were also changed or omitted at the woman's request.

One thing for which I was unprepared was the emotion unleashed by women unused to talking at length about themselves and their experiences. Many wept during the interview, even those who had not suffered directly from the violent repression. Years of rule by repressive regimes, and the authorities' pervasive use of informers at all levels of society, has resulted in decades of silence for many Guatemalan women. This means that when they speak about anything 'controversial', they are afraid of being overheard. This fear pervades even the intimacy of their homes. In many cases my tape recorder had to be placed very close to the speaker in order to pick up a voice kept intentionally low. But there was also laughter in our conversations, and a particular empathy when we talked about the concerns that all women have in common, such as fertility and sexuality. Many of the women said that these were issues they had never talked about before.

While I was doing the interviews, I realised that many of these women were taking a considerable risk by telling me certain things. As one of the women interviewed here says, '... in Guatemala, anybody who asks for a salary rise or says that hunger or illiteracy exists, is accused of being a communist.'

I thought of all the Guatemalan women who have been tortured, assassinated and 'disappeared', and the important and dangerous work that many Guatemalan women are undertaking today: Nineth, one of the leaders of the Gam (Mutual Support Group), for whom death threats are an everyday occurrence; the Indian women of Conavigua (the National Co-ordinating Committee of Guatemalan Widows), constantly harassed by the army; the women trade unionists of the Unsitragua federation who wondered if they would still be alive when this book came out; the nun in Coban who single-handedly defied army attempts to break into a convent where she was caring for internal refugees: and the thousands of brave Guatemalan women who, in a myriad of ways, daily defy the authorities' attempts to control their lives.

There are also the women who are courageous in less obvious ways: Luz, who brought wrath on her head for her outspoken defence of women's reproductive rights; Isabel de los Angeles, the poet who fought sexual discrimination in the 1960s and was forced to abandon a brilliant career, but who continues to write and sell her poems on the street; and Enma, Margarita and Manuela, Indian women who, by challenging women's role in their communities and refusing to compromise, have put their emotional security at risk.

The women in this collection of interviews have given so much to this, their book — their stories, their ideas and their trust. They allow us to enter their world and to glimpse the reality of a woman's life in Guatemala.

Margaret Hooks
Tepoztlán, Mexico
September 1991

1
EARNING
A
LIVING

On the finca

Every winter, Indians from the highland areas of Guatemala leave their cool mountain valleys to work on the enormous coastal coffee and cotton plantations from which the Guatemalan elite gains most of its wealth. Unable to exist on their own tiny plots, which one Latin American writer has described as being no bigger than a grave, thousands of Guatemalan *campesinos* migrate to work on these *fincas*. Women make up a large percentage of this temporary workforce, earning about US$2 or £1.18 a day.

In addition to their work in the fields, the women usually have to care for their children in virtually subhuman conditions. Temporary workers are housed in long, open-sided sheds with dirt floors and no furniture. They seldom have access to toilets or piped water. Infant mortality is high and many women lose one or more of their children as a result of the unsanitary conditions and the uncontrolled use of pesticides in the *fincas*.

Margarita is a *Cakchiquel* Indian from Chimaltenango who spent her youth working on these plantations. Now 30 years old and single, she is working as a live-in servant for a North American family in Guatemala City. Her home village is about three hours from Guatemala City and is only accessible on foot or by jeep; she returns there to visit her family about once a month. The army is much in evidence in the area and there are many widows. Margarita, who belongs to an Evangelical sect, prefers not to talk about the violence that has taken place there. Although she has lived in the capital for several years, she still feels strong ties to her community and continues to weave and wear the traditional *traje* of her village.

My father died when I was very young and my mother had to find a way of feeding and clothing us, so we made *huipiles* and baskets. When I was about ten years old I started gathering and selling blackberries for money to buy thread for the *huipiles*.

Then when I was 13 we set up a little grocery shop in the house and I learned how to add up — I couldn't multiply very well but I knew how much everything cost. This only lasted six months and then I had to go to work on a coffee *finca*.

I went for three months towards the end of every year — to pick coffee if possible, if not, to clear the fields after the other pickers. We had to get up at three o'clock in the morning to make breakfast and walk the long way to the coffee fields, arriving by seven o'clock in the morning. We had to to get there early in order to finish the work by one o'clock, when it's getting too hot to do anything.

At two o'clock they would sound the loudspeaker so that we would leave the fields and get what we had cut weighed. We had to carry the bags of coffee on our backs. The strongest men carried 100 pounds, and so did the women who had the strength. I could only carry 60 pounds.

There were always long queues at the place where they weighed the coffee. If a woman was with her husband or brothers, then the men would wait to do the weighing and the woman could go on ahead to prepare something to eat. But if she didn't have anyone to help her, then she would have to wait too, even though she would sometimes have to go back after dark. This is one of the problems of single women working on a *finca*. It's frightening walking around after dark. If you have other women friends you can make an arrangement with them and all go together, but if you have no friends or family you feel very alone.

We were all housed together in long sheds — there's no privacy. About 40 to 50 people, sleeping in groups. One night I woke up at about midnight and felt a man on top of me. I hit him hard and screamed but none of the other people helped me. I had to take care of myself.

When you get back to the sheds in the evening you have to wash your clothes and go for the *tortillas*. The only thing they gave us to eat was *tortillas* and beans. Sixteen *tortillas* a day: eight in the morning and eight in the evening.

In one *finca* where I picked coffee there was no running water so they kept the water in drums that had been used to store petrol, and then they used this water to make our *tortillas*. We had to eat *tortillas* that tasted of petrol. It was awful, but we were hungry. There was no water anywhere there, no rivers, no drinking water;

3

only a trickle in a gully but it smelt of skunk. We had to get right into the gully to collect it, and the smell of skunk, ugh!

On Sundays we had a day off. We were given a small advance on our wages to buy potatoes or a bit of meat and then we prepared our own meals. You get so tired of beans, beans, beans. So on Sundays you make stew, even though it's a very long walk to the butchers.

The one thing I couldn't stand about the *finca* was the dirt. Picking the coffee wasn't so bad, but there were no toilets — not even a ditch where we could go. I really noticed the dirt, there were flies on the *tortilla* dough, on the dishes, everywhere. So much poverty that it was depressing. Some people were aware of the situation and were careful to move away from the rest of us if they needed to go to the toilet, but others didn't care and went anywhere. There must have been a lot of germs, and people became sick with fevers and coughs.

Another horrible thing is fumigation, but this only happened to me when I was picking cotton, not coffee. They never warned us beforehand, they would just cover the food. But the smell of the poison was very, very, strong — dreadful — and when the planes passed overhead it fell on us, leaving marks on our hands, like milk, some kind of liquid...

You never see the owners of these *fincas.* They don't even come to pay you. There's a foreman. People would say, 'Hurry up, get a move on. Here he comes'. There are good and bad foremen — some will help the women to reach the coffee on the topmost branches but others (and our own people are sometimes the worst) only ill-treat you.

The reason I went to work on the *fincas* was to pay for fertiliser. Since my family has only a little plot of land, and we didn't have the cash to buy fertiliser, we had to get it on credit from the contractor. He gave a hundredweight to each of us and then we had to pay off the debt by going to work on the *finca*. The contractor works for the *finca* owner. At times we earned enough to pay back our debt and have a little bit over to buy clothes.

What I would really like to have been is a nurse, because I see that when the children here in the city go to a doctor they get better really quickly. This is very different to what happens to the children in my village. There is a health centre there, but when I go back I see many sick children. So I ask, 'Why don't you go to the health

4

centre?', and the people say, 'There's nobody there, it's closed'. And if someone is there, I ask the people, 'What medicine did they give you?' 'An aspirin', one of them says. 'And you?' I ask another, 'An aspirin'. And I wonder whether they all have the same illness that they're all being given aspirin! But I know this isn't so, because some have coughs, some fevers and so on. It would be better for them to go to a private doctor, but they don't have the money. When I see how quickly children are cured here in the capital, with a few drops or pills, I see that children are dying for lack of money. So I would like to help them. It would be great, if I had the money, to open up a chemist's shop in the village. At the moment there isn't one and people have to go a long way, to the nearest town... I'm willing to work but I don't have the funds.

Lady of the coffee plantation

The beans for your morning cup of coffee may well have been grown on the enormous plantations of Guatemala's most conservative sector: the coffee exporters. On estates reputed to be amongst the largest in the world, a handful of families control about 80 per cent of Guatemala's main export crop and principal foreign exchange earner. Traditionally resistant to change, the coffee producers have rejected, often violently, any attempt to bring about even minor agrarian reform. Many of them have found both representation and voice in the self-proclaimed 'party of organised violence', the ultra-right National Liberation Movement, linked to the notorious Guatemalan death squads.

Amparo, a *ladina* born to Spanish parents, is from a coffee-producing family. She is in her 70s, and her sons now manage the enormous *finca* that she often ran in her late husband's absence. According to published reports, her husband was so feared for his cruelty that Indians living in the area referred to him as 'the Tiger of Ixcan'. His notoriety led a Guatemalan guerrilla organisation, the Guerrilla Army of the Poor (EGP), to single him out for execution. This was carried out on his own *finca* in 1975. In retaliation, the Guatemalan army abducted 37 leaders of peasant cooperatives, who were never seen again.

I was born in Quetzaltenango but soon afterwards my parents took me to Spain. I grew up there, and came back to Guatemala when I was 19. A year later I married a Guatemalan of Colombian origin.

I started work on the *finca* at my husband's side. But he would often be out in the fields and I would stay in the house. I never felt lonely because I had very good servants. When my husband had to go to Guatemala City I stayed behind and supervised the workers. I would send the coffee on mules to Nebaj, where it was loaded onto a bus to go to the capital.

We had a very nice house with many patios. It had six bedrooms. We never had time to make it as pretty as we had planned. And, although I had come from Europe, I got used to this way of life.

Usually, I would get up at about 7 o'clock and have breakfast with my sons and husband, if he was there. We breakfasted very well. We had cows, so there was milk. There was fresh bread: the women who worked there, the older ones especially, knew how to bake bread. So, we had bread, eggs, beans, fried bananas. After that we would ride around the *finca* on horseback.

My husband penetrated further into the jungle of the Ixcan, to what is today called Playa Grande, and he saw that there was rubber. As this was during the war, this was very important for tyres. A North American company gave him the equipment to extract the rubber, so he went off to do that and I stayed on the *finca*, running it myself.

I was very happy there, but my husband became involved in politics and he often had to leave the country or was in prison and I had to run the *finca* by myself. We had a lot of problems, everything became really difficult. So I left the *finca* and didn't return for a long time.

My husband stayed on, but nothing was the same: my marriage, nothing ... In the end I got divorced for economic reasons: all the money from the *finca* was going into politics. Politics is fine, but not when you have a wife and five children to look after. My husband founded an anti-Communist party ... It's not good, your husband being involved in all of this.

He had a very harsh character, but he was good to his people. They killed my husband. It was when he went to pay the people their wages once. The *finca* had grown a lot, it was lovely, the coffee fields, the streams — the church had still not been built. He was paying people when suddenly six or seven men arrived. 'We have come to kill the Tiger', they said, and just like that they killed him. It was horrible. They didn't steal any of the money, but they shot him down. He was buried on the *finca*. After this my sons took over the *finca*.

We don't have any labour problems, the *finca* has electricity and very good machinery. People have their little houses, and they live well. More than a thousand people live and work on the *finca*. It is enormous. Most of the land is wild and very fertile because there are many rivers and it rains a lot. We used to transport goods by mule; nowadays, we move around in light planes.

The people who work on the *finca* are Indians. I have never had any problems with them; they are good people. The women have a lot of children — 10, 11, 12, 14 and many of them die. People are Catholic, but what sort of Catholicism is it? They are Catholics, but they baptise their children and nothing else. There are no priests in this area. Early on there was no church, but we had one built and some American Evangelicals are now constructing a hospital.

People here love me so much that I took part in a birth on the *finca*, and I don't know anything about medicine! It wasn't one of the Indian women who was giving birth, it was the wife of one of the overseers... I have always been very concerned about my people. There is a school on the *finca* and we always try to help anyone who is sick. For example, on one occasion when there was a government amnesty for guerrillas, over 2,000 people arrived at the *finca* in a very bad state, very ill and really thin. They had been in the mountains. They were asked why they had gone with the guerrillas and they said that they had been told that Guatemala was going to be theirs, that the crops would be theirs, the light planes, everything. But there was none of that. There they were in the mountains and all they had to eat were plants, no salt, and their clothes were ruined. When the army went after them they had to hide, and many children died. So they came to the *finca*. We built them houses — well, one big shed for all of them. They were given corn, beans, salt, coffee and molasses, pretty good, eh? But when they ate the salt they began to die, because of the fluid retention. Then the Evangelicals got in touch with one of my sons to see if we would allow them to come to cure the refugees. My son told them to come and cure not just the refugees but all of the sick. They came, and they are still on the *finca* but the refugees have been taken away to a village somewhere else.

There is a lot of social work to be done in Guatemala, without a doubt. I think we must all get together and form committees so that there are fewer illiterate people and fewer starving children. Nowadays I belong to a group called the Sisters of Mercy, and I am co-ordinator of a little school here called the Grace of God. I wish that there were more people in Guatemala who would take an interest in these things.

The economic situation is not good. This government redistribution of land is a very complicated issue. It's not just a question of taking away a *finca* and giving it to someone else. You give them the land and what do they do with it? They can't do anything. Once a group of people came to cultivate this part of the

Ixcan. They did it half-wittedly and without any organisation. They sowed corn and got a really good crop and then what happened? They couldn't transport it out. How could they get it out if there are no roads? We take our coffee out in planes because coffee pays well — but corn? It's worth nothing! You can't air freight it. So the corn just rotted.

These people don't want virgin land that they would have to work. When I first came to the *finca* there wasn't anything — no road, no doctor, no medicine. So why don't they do the same? You know why? Because they have no proper management.

I have learnt what it is to love land. If you come to love the land then it doesn't matter what sacrifices you have to make, as long as you save the land. There is a point at which profit is not so important. What is important is your land, your people. I have my roots in the land. I would say that I am an agriculturist. I love the land, I am profoundly Catholic, I have great faith in God, and I am a mother. My religion has given me pleasure and hope. My family is my reality, but the land is my roots. I went to see the film *Gone with the Wind* and I understood it very well. My life has been a bit like that film.

When my children were young I wrote this poem about the *finca*:

Land of ours
spiritual beauty
which omnipotent God wished to bequeath us
land and God
abundant and splendid
magnificent and serene
situated between the mountains and solitude.
Cradle of my children
market place of a race that overflows with America's strength
faithful servants...

In the market-place

The colourful street markets of Latin America feature on virtually every tourist's itinerary. In Guatemala, visitors delight in the exotic foods on display and are thrilled at the prospect of finding a bargain among the hundreds of curios that are available. Seldom do they look beyond the riot of colour, smell and noise at the careworn faces of many of the market women — women for whom a sale can mean the difference between being able to feed their families or not.

Most food market traders are women. Often they are limited to selling items of lesser value — fruit, vegetables and bread rather than meat, fish, and cheese. Further down the pecking order are those women who sell items such as secondhand clothing and metal 'junk' to the poorest sectors of their societies. Usually they cannot afford to rent a stall so they spread out their few goods on the pavement.

In Guatemala City, the municipal authorities have stated that they want to be rid of these sellers, claiming that they clutter the footpaths, make it difficult for people to park their cars and that their wares are unsightly. But the women sellers refuse to go, arguing that their trade brings in money that is vital if they are to support their families.

Market women are traditionally vocal in Central America and often play a key role in social protest. The strong sense of community prevalent in markets has promoted organisation and unity — organisation that has sometimes been met with brutal repression.

In 1988, the women at the Plaza Quemada market, in a rather run-down and seedy part of Guatemala City, were involved in a dispute with the city mayor over their right to sell on the pavement. Doña Irma, a *ladina* representative of these women, was interviewed when she and other women visited a trade union organisation to ask for support during the dispute.

I was born in Guatemala City. My mother grew up in the old Central market. She worked as a guide taking North Americans around the

10

market, then she moved to the Plaza Quemada. She worked in markets all her life and she brought me up in them as well.

I've been working in markets for about 40 years. I'm 46 years old, and I've been selling since I was a kid. Like most of the women who work at the Plaza Quemada I sell second-hand clothes, old shoes and bits of junk. A few of the women sell fruit, pineapples and watermelon. Early in the morning I go out to the suburbs and knock on people's doors, asking them to sell me the old clothes and shoes that they don't wear anymore. I take buses to get from one place to another. I sell from about midday until about 7 o'clock in the evening. I practically grew up in this business.

Now the mayor doesn't want us to sell in the street — but we have to, because we are very poor. These mayors make us suffer. One after another, they all have different ideas. We managed to come to an agreement with the others, but this one is different. He says he wants the streets cleaned up completely.

There aren't just a few of us. There are thousands of us who work in street markets, and we have been organised for more than eight years. I am one of the representatives. We have a strong sense of community, and when we started to have problems I said to the other women that we should form a group so that we would be stronger and could persuade the authorities to let us carry on selling. We are petitioning them now. They say that they don't want delinquency, but if they don't let us work then what can we do? If you can't work you turn to crime. We are trying to mind our own business and sell.

It's not as if the authorities are giving us something for nothing; if they were, they could take it away. We are paying for the public right of way. We are in the street, out in the open air, we have no protection and yet still they charge us. Some of us pay the council up to two *quetzales* a metre each day for our places on the pavement; the minimum is about 80 cents. It depends on the amount of space you take up. Now the authorities are saying that we will have to pay seven *quetzales* a metre. We can't pay that because sometimes we sell and sometimes we don't. Sometimes we go home with nothing. We don't have enough security to be able to pay seven *quetzales*. In the rainy season we sell hardly anything. It's disastrous because we don't have any covering overhead and we are outdoors. When it rains we put a piece of plastic over our things and take shelter in shop doorways until it stops. During the

11

dry season and when sales are constant I make between five and ten *quetzales* a day. I work virtually every day of the week, including Sundays.

Life is a grind

The biggest problem facing us women today is the terrible economic situation. Before, we could buy everything we needed with five to ten *quetzales*, but not any more. We can no longer eat meat — a pound of poor quality meat costs three *quetzales*.

Many of the sellers are women on their own. Their husbands have 'disappeared', and they are left with young children. These women *must* work, they have to support their kids. Some days the poorer women don't have anything to sell, at times there are women who have only two or three pairs of old shoes to sell.

I have five children to support and send to school and I have to buy them pencils and notebooks and whatever the schools require. These are very expensive. My husband doesn't earn much, as he mends shoes. We try to live on his tiny income, but there are seven of us and we can't survive on it. What I earn only buys some beans and bread because nowadays five *quetzales* is nothing ... Sometimes we don't even have one *quetzal* to buy bread, never mind the more expensive things.

We can't afford to rent a house. The seven of us live in one room, with a little kitchenette. We pay 25 *quetzales* rent. It's not very elegant, but at least we are not in the street — we have a roof over our heads.

It's because of our poverty that I want my children to be something later on. Not university-educated or lawyers or anything like that, but able to look after themselves and find a job. I don't want my kids to end up in the markets. That is precisely why I'm involved in organising the market traders over our rights, because I don't want my children to carry the same cross as I have.

I'm sorry now that I never went to school, that I don't know anything. My parents were too poor, and I didn't care. Also, in those days parents didn't put much emphasis on self-improvement. I regret that I don't know how to read or write because it's very useful, but I'm too old now — although some of my friends say that it's never too late.

Life is a grind these days and who knows what it will be like when my children are adults. You always want the best for your children. But if the authorities won't let us work, how can we pay for our children's studies? They close off all other paths to us, they want there to be more delinquency. After all, if a child doesn't go to school what does he do? He becomes a delinquent. So I keep telling my children that everybody has to work, that there is no such thing as degrading work. Selling newspapers is not degrading, nor is cleaning people's shoes.

The rich don't have any problems. They eat when they want to. They have their pint of milk, they eat the best meat there is and the best eggs. They are taken more notice of than we poor people. Yet they still provoke us when they come to their big shops and want to park their cars. 'Get rid of this rubbish', they say to us, referring to our wares. 'Pavements are for parking cars beside, not for you to sit on'. But they have homes and we are poor; they earn in a short time what it takes us months to earn. Yet it's all the same to them whether we sell or not, and whether we eat or not. They say that it's been difficult for them to get to where they've got to, and it's true, it has. But they don't need to humiliate us. We are human, too.

I think everybody is equal. The difference is that those who have had an education are lucky, and they should have more of a conscience. But they don't, they crush you if they can. They'd rather be able to park their cars than let me sell goods to provide for my children.

I sell beauty

Most notable in Guatemala is the contrast between the 'haves' and the 'have-nots'. Heavily guarded, wealthy neighbourhoods with rooftops bristling with satellite dishes back on to sprawling shantytowns of one-room shacks where clean water is a luxury. A relatively small group of extremely wealthy landowners and business people rule Guatemala. A mere five per cent of the population receives nearly 60 per cent of the country's total income.

Once described by a US congressman as 'without much in the way of redeeming features', Guatemala's ruling class appears to be either out of touch with, or immune to, the real situation of most of its compatriots. Many of this elite are first or second generation Guatemalans, usually of Spanish or German descent, and the best that Guatemala's poor can expect from them is grudging paternalism.

Yvette lives in such a suburb. In her late 50s and of German descent, her home reflects her wealth. Enormous oil paintings and French furniture are displayed inside, cars with blacked-out windows and bodyguards wait outside. Her family owns several *fincas* and she works in the field of women's 'intimate wear'. She also sells imported beauty products, just one of which costs almost the equivalent of a year's average rural wage.

I was born in Guatemala City. I am very proud of being Guatemalan. I am very happily married. My husband was a banker; today he's an enthusiastic businessman. We have five children, all professionals — amongst them are business administrators, educated in Boston, and an industrial engineer. My youngest daughter is a beauty director and a qualified stylist.

Two generations back, my family arrived from Germany. I feel a lot of admiration for the German people. I think that that is where we get our business acumen from, because my family were successful business people in Germany. I enjoy business. People ask me if I still work, because my children are all working now —

I tell them I'll die working. I still go to the office every day. I am the executive vice-president. It's a lot of responsibility but I like it. More than anything I like seeing how the designs are going to come out.

I've read a lot of biographies, and I would love to be like Helena Rubenstein or Elizabeth Arden. Elizabeth Arden was opening beauty clinics until she was 85 years old! These two great ladies of beauty inspire me.

The career a woman chooses is very important for her country, whether it be a doctor, a writer, a lawyer or a businesswoman. Each of us fulfils herself in the field she chooses. I like the beauty field and I have evolved and fulfilled myself in it by producing and distributing high quality beauty products that have proved to be effective in beautifying women. That's why in the beauty field we say there is no such thing as an ugly woman.

I feel good when I see that the product I provide for someone satisfies her needs. I know that it will improve her looks because, really, a woman who is discreetly made-up and who uses her night cream looks and feels better. And this will help her get ahead. It's wonderful, because the face, the skin, is the passport to a good business, to selling more and improving yourself in every way. One really does prefer to see a well done-up woman to one who isn't.

I have also fulfilled myself in the field of interior beauty, in making day and night intimate wear: brassieres, slips, panties, nightdresses and pyjamas. If you are wearing good, well-fitting underwear your dresses look better and you feel better. You could say that I sell beauty — both internal and external.

We produce these two lines of beauty products in Guatemala and distribute them throughout Central America. Exports are very important because they bring foreign currency to Guatemala. We employ approximately 350 people, so we are providing work for a lot of Guatemalans. We employ about 140 seamstresses: women who have a lot of problems, but we have two well-trained sociologists and a psychologist in the company who are continuously helping them.

The basic thing for any woman in any profession is to have a lot of self confidence and, of course, training, experience, education. Another very important thing is tranquillity in the home. The more content you are in your home with your husband and children, the more you are able to produce. So my advice to women is: put your family first. If you are successful in business but your family is a disaster, you won't be happy. As far as I've been able, I've always put my family before my business. If they are not happy, I am not happy.

In the 32 years since I formed my business, I've never suffered any discrimination for being a woman. On the contrary, I've been admired by both men and women because I was one of the first businesswomen in Guatemala, and they were pleased when I entered the field. Also, if people see you are self-assured, positive, and knowledgeable about your product, you can easily become successful. It seems that Guatemalan women are excelling more every day. There are more professionals, more women going to university and more in business, the arts and politics. This really thrills me. Whenever I can, I try to help my employees. I say, 'Go to university! Educate yourself and study so you can get ahead.'

I love Indians
The poor woman is very self-sacrificing, especially the indigenous woman. She has to work day and night at her husband's side in order to survive. She has to weave and sell things to support the family. She has to do her domestic chores, make the food, attend to her husband and children, make the *tortillas* and take her husband's lunch to wherever he is working. The life of the Indian woman and the non-Indian poor woman is very hard.

It's a question of education. I think we should try and make both men and women attend school to learn to read. If they can read, they can get ahead. Although there are Indians who don't know how to read or write who have successful businesses... It's innate in them. Indian women buy weavings and handicrafts and sell them in the market. They do business even without speaking Spanish — and they do well. You know, I believe that any woman can excel, regardless of her social status. She only has to want to. You don't need to be educated to be a good businesswoman. On our *finca* we sell eggs to the Indian women at three *quetzales* a dozen and they take them to the market and sell them for four. So, with the sale of four dozen they make four *quetzales*, which is something. It gives me great pleasure to be able to help them.

Something that has been very important to me ever since we founded the company is that we've tried to help the Indians of Guatemala. We have taken on people from the Chimaltenango area and they've turned out well. Take the case of a young boy who came here. He didn't have anywhere to sleep, so he worked as a watchman, cleaning the house and the pool. Little by little he got ahead, he studied accounting, and today he has an important post in the company.

I love Indians, all Indians, but especially the ones from Chimaltenango. We have noticed that they work better, they are more interested, and they focus all their attention on the task assigned to them.

Being Catholic

Religion is also very, very, very important to me. I am a Catholic. I was born a Catholic, and will be Catholic all my life. We go to church when necessary, but deeds are more important. I always ask God for success in the business and to be able to help our people, our employees, because the better the company is the better their salaries will be, and the more we can help them. One of my daily requests is that we will sell and produce more. I am very devout and have a lot of faith in God. I believe that God has helped me enormously in my business. Often when I have certain ideas, business ideas, when I want to introduce new products, I trust in God that I will be successful — and I am.

The picture of health

The vast majority of the rural population of Guatemala is unable ever to consult a doctor. Access to hospitals is even more limited: only one hospital bed is available for every 500 Guatemalans. Most of them would be unable to afford hospital care even if it were available.

Health care is a luxury in this nation where, in a single day, 115 children under the age of five die as result of easily preventable diseases. Women and children are most affected: infant and maternal mortality rates in Guatemala are the highest in Central America. Many of these deaths could be prevented by adequate medical care, proper sewage facilities and clean water.

Faced with the lack of adequate care facilities, communities have attempted to look after their own health needs as best they can. Midwives and local *curanderos* (healers) have traditionally formed the backbone of most rural health care. Their knowledge and capabilities with regard to traditional, or natural, medicine is extensive, but they are unable to provide complete medical attention. As a result, in recent years there has been an increase in the training of 'health promoters'. These are usually members of the local population who receive basic training in modern medicine to prepare them for work in their own communities. They are then able to bring some of the benefits of western-style medicine to rural areas, and to supplement the work of the local *curanderos*.

Yolanda, a 25-year-old *Cakchiquel* Indian, is a qualified nurse who works in a programme training health promoters. This training focuses on preparing promoters to promote good health rather than just cure the sick.

Promoting health in rural areas frequently means getting involved in the community's demands for better living conditions. In Guatemala, this type of activity is often branded as subversive, and many health promoters have paid with their lives for such involvement.

As soon as I qualified as a primary school teacher I was sent to my village to give literacy classes. I really wanted to study medicine, however, because I could see that health was a big problem. But my father told me that he couldn't afford to send me back to school because he had to educate my brothers and I would have to contribute. Anyway, as I was a woman, the first thing I would do was get married. But a foreign priest whom I knew encouraged me and offered to support me so that I could study nursing. My dream was to study medicine, but I'm happy being a nurse.

When I was at nursing college, I felt uneasy at the prospect of working in hospitals because I sometimes felt marginalised. I didn't create this marginalisation. The head of the nursing school had told me that if I wanted to continue to wear my *traje*, I could. I didn't want to wear the *trajes* that I wore at home to work, because of the risk of infection. But I didn't have a lot of clothes, just two outfits, so I wore one, washed the other one, and alternated like that. I soon realised that some of the nurses and doctors igonored me when they saw me dressed in *traje*. But I decided that the *traje* is mine; it is part of my life, I can't abandon it. It isn't the *traje* that makes me a nurse or not, but how well I can help people.

Although I concentrated on my studies and on my relationship with the patients, I still wasn't happy working at the hospital. I felt much better when I left and went to work in indigenous communities. I felt drawn towards community health, and I had teachers who pushed me and encouraged me. I have to thank them. They were all *ladinas*, but they really helped me. Then I heard about this job training health promoters.

If you are poor and ill, you'd be better off dead

The health situation in Guatemala is very bad, especially from the point of view of the poor, who cannot afford medical consultations or medicines. The government health centres do not treat them well — often they have no medical supplies anyway. The only things available are private clinics, and they charge a fortune.

The health services are centralised and many people have to travel for miles to get to them. For example, all the specialist hospitals are in the same area, which means that for most people just getting to the hospital is very expensive. It's a very serious problem. If you are poor and get ill you'd be better off dead, rather than wasting your time going through the whole rigmarole. Health cannot be separated from political, social and economic conditions — definitely not. I can't say to people, 'Look, eat properly; I will teach you about the nutritive value of different foods', when they don't have the money to buy them.

The organisation that I work with trains about 200 health promoters. The course has four levels. We teach how health should be perceived, how we should work together, what strategies should be employed to achieve health and (although this is a big challenge) how we can attain health for everyone when social and structural change takes place in Guatemala — because it cannot be attained in any other way.

The health promoter focuses on two areas. One of them is curing: if someone is ill, I have to cure him or her. However, we put more emphasis on the other focus: prevention. And by that I don't mean just carrying out vaccinations or promoting breast feeding.

The basis of all health work is organisation. If a community is not organised and is unclear about the underlying causes of ill health, then it is impossible to carry out projects that will be of benefit to most people. We try to make people think and be practical. We use a very participatory methodology, whereby the promoters get to know their own real needs. We also try to avoid encouraging 'small activities', preferring to work to a plan with a clear goal. Today the promoter may be working with someone who is ill, but he should be thinking, 'Why don't I work more with groups? Why don't we create projects together that not only talk about microbes in the water, but encourage the whole community to launch a plan to get clean drinking water? So that the community knows it has the right to clean water and land.'

It has to be part of a process. You start with the minimum and in the long run you achieve more, not just for a small group, or a couple of families, but for a whole community. It's a slow process, which is why at the initial level we concentrate on finding points that the promoters' communities have in common. At the second level we put more emphasis on the health situation. By the third level, the situation is much clearer and the fourth level is where the promoters decide what they want to achieve in their own communities. We provide them with guidelines and they attempt to carry out their own projects. The idea is that they themselves decide what they really want to achieve.

We want to use a mixture of western and traditional medicine. Not all western medicine is bad *per se*. There are very good things about western medicine, but there must also be a re-evaluation of the medicine that our communities have practised for centuries. Many excellent health practices should be rescued because they are still of use — not all traditional medicine, because it's not all good, but there are things that can be revived — and health professionals cannot do this if they do not have political clarity. If they cannot comprehend the situation, they cannot evaluate it.

Health professionals prefer western medicine because selling drugs and healing the sick is more lucrative. The more specialised you are the more you earn. It is a system that favours professionals. Traditional medicine is not really like that. It is more about sharing and helping one another, and if you are paid it's related to how much the patient can afford. You don't say, 'You owe me so much because I did such and such'. In the indigenous communities, you always say, 'It's up to you how much you give.'

Health professionals, including my fellow nurses, are one of the greatest obstacles to health in Guatemala, because they have no idea of the reality of people's lives. When they are preparing their programmes they always focus on a very western-style medicine. The trips that I made around the country enabled me to see how each of the health promoters lived and the health situation in their communities. This helped me to see that I could not continue to regard health from a simplistic viewpoint. It has to be seen within a political and social context, it must be studied from its roots. Illness does not exist just because of germs, it is a result of certain social conditions.

When I teach I feel obliged to make the truth known from various angles. I suspect that when I approach the area of popular education, other professionals don't look kindly on what I do. I fear that it is viewed as subversive. For this reason we also discuss with the health promoters what measures we should take to prevent atrocities recurring. In past years, health promoters were killed as part of the army's counter-insurgency plans. This must not happen again.

Women's health
Going down the health scale here we find that women and children

are worst off. And why are women so affected? Because of the *machismo* in Guatemala.

The woman has less opportunity of getting out of the house and less possibility of going to school. She is looked upon with contempt and, as a result, not only does she not take care of herself, she also neglects her family. *Machismo* affects all women, both *ladinas* and indigenous, but it affects the latter more. Not only does the man not allow her to leave the home, but because the racial discrimination is so enormous Indian women are incapable of conceiving of better health benefits for themselves or their children. They are maltreated in health centres because they cannot speak Spanish and are unable to explain what their problem is.

Women need to be provided with skills and I think the way to achieve this is by treating the couple as an entity. Get the woman out of the house and make the man understand that she has a right to improve herself. The family is part and parcel of the woman's chains because she is obliged to stay at home and care for the children. Simply by venturing out of the house, a woman takes a big step.

There are more men than women among the health promoters, but this doesn't bother me. I find it a way of making the men think about women's worth, and I introduce questions that provoke us to discuss and analyse women's rights.

Within our group work, we always try to motivate the women in the community to choose the promoter, whether it be a man or a woman. We are gradually increasing the number of women in training. It used to be about one woman in a group of 15 men, now it's about five women to ten men.

A very important factor here in Guatemala is the midwives who have become community leaders — much more so than health promoters have ever been. I have been pushing for more midwives to become leaders and work for the health of the community.

The dangers involved

The Indian struggle is very complex because it is not only about overcoming poverty, it is also about racism. The indigenous sector is the hardest hit and has fewest resources. This disparity that has been imposed upon us will have to disappear. Indians as well as *ladinos* must fight for a more just life, because we too have a right to life, a right to health.

I hope that one day we will live in a more just society, so I want to teach people things that will be useful to them. I am teaching myself through them as well, and I believe that we are growing together. We need social change in Guatemala, and that is the point of departure I take in my work.

Many people have told me that this work is very risky, but I can't just give it up and go and work in a hospital. I couldn't live thinking of those who are suffering while I just keep quiet. I couldn't do it. To me it would be the greatest sin that I could commit.

One of my problems at the moment is my family. Their dream is that I should get married because it's getting late. I'm 25 and they are afraid I might miss the boat. I have told my mother that marriage doesn't concern me much at this point... I feel fine being single because I can get around better and I don't have to worry about children. Also, my biggest problem is there are few men who could understand my work. I'm not a woman who concentrates on the home, I'm often away giving talks here and there, I go on trips, I work within a group, focusing on other people. Few men understand... It's a conflict, but my family understands my work now, even when I have to be away for two weeks at a time. It has been difficult, but I have helped them to understand by explaining exactly what I do and by being honest. Now they support what I am doing. They feel afraid for me, they tell me to be careful and not to talk to just anybody. I tell them that this is the way my life is, and if some day I 'disappear' they will have to understand that I would have died one day anyway... I want them to come to terms with my life, so that in the end it will not be such a hard blow and they will understand why it happened.

I've given my best years to the United States

In recent years there has been a sharp increase in Guatemalans entering the United States for political reasons, but previously the overwhelming reasons for such migrations were economic. Hundreds of thousands of Guatemalans unable to earn a decent wage in their own country embarked upon a costly, and often risky, 3,000 mile odyssey. Most ended up as illegal workers in the United States, doing jobs that most North Americans consider beneath them.

Lydia is a *ladina* in her late 50s who has worked in the United States as a domestic servant for nearly 20 years. She comes from Chiquimula in eastern Guatemala, a hot, arid and primarily *ladino* part of the country renowned for its violence, its *machismo*, and the frankness and brusqueness of its inhabitants. All of Lydia's immediate family except for one son still live in Guatemala.

I was born in Chiquimula. They call it the 'Pearl of the Orient'. My grandmother brought me up there and when she died my mother took us to Izabal, also in the east of Guatemala. I got married at 13 and had my first child when I was 15. I had one every year after that until I had five. When my eldest was 15, I separated from my husband and went to live in Guatemala City. I went to work in a clothing factory and tried my best to educate my kids.

I don't know why I married so young. I had no idea what making love was about. I didn't know that my husband could be as bad as he was good. I thought I was going to be the one to give the orders and be the lady of the house. I had this vision of having a nice house with my children going off to school every day. But I had no idea of how I was going to have these children, nor what I would have to go through to bring them up.

I would like to have been a nurse but because I married so young I only went to primary school. Even so, my family had some good connections and a doctor offered me the chance of learning laboratory work at the hospital, which would have meant living away from home. I had two children at the time, but when I told my husband he said it was fine with him. The truth is he was a real womaniser and wanted me out of the house so that he would have more freedom.

This hadn't occurred to me, but one of his women started telling her friends that my husband was only waiting for me to leave so that he could bring her to the house. I realised that if I left he would move her in and I'd be left on my own with the children. So in order to keep him I said that I wouldn't go, but I regretted it.

To be honest I don't know when I've ever been happy. It has always been a mixture of happiness and bitterness. I felt happy when we had parties. My husband liked socialising and he used to organise very lively parties with good marimba bands from Guatemala City. He liked to dance and that was the one thing that made me happy: dancing ... But my heart was in pieces seeing my husband at the other side of the room with another woman. I could see what he was doing but I wouldn't say anything because I couldn't lower myself. I didn't want anyone to know what I was suffering, and I thought it was shameful to fight over a man. So I laughed and passed around the food, or ate what was offered me, but the food stuck in my throat.

I am a very affectionate woman and I wanted my husband to be affectionate with me, too, so I tried to show him how. I'd say to him, 'Look at this, sweetheart; did you see that, love? Let's do this, and that'. And he'd reply, 'It's your thing; do it if you want to. I'm tired.' But I didn't care if he was tired, I wasn't, and I tried to get him to do things. I'd put on my trousers and go bike riding, or ride mules. I loved it — I was like a man. I cut corn and picked beans and chopped down bananas. I worked hard.

I don't know why I tried to keep him. It only meant having more children and in the end I separated from him anyway. Now I always tell other women they shouldn't try to keep their husbands. We shouldn't force them to stay with us. They come back for a while, but then they go off again. That's the way he was. He would go with another woman until I found out, and then he would leave her. But he'd find another one later. It's not worth wasting your life trying to keep a man — if you are still young you should leave him, and maybe you'll be able to find someone else who will make you happier. After all, who's going to want you after you have had a ton of kids...

I don't think it's a good idea for women to have a lot of children these days. I had mine because I was young and didn't know any better. I don't totally agree with abortion but I do believe in using contraception. I have never used it because I don't need to now — they tied my tubes. It happened back in Guatemala when I ran a stall selling beer and soft drinks. Every other day I would have to unload over 100 crates from the train and onto a tractor, and then carry them in to the house. This damaged my womb and I was bleeding for seven months. They couldn't find out what it was so they decided to operate. Two of the doctors were cousins of mine and they said, 'This woman lives with a man who doesn't appreciate her and who runs about all over the place. It's not worth her having any more children, so we should tie her tubes...' They didn't give me the chance to agree or not because I was under anaesthetic at the time. They only told me what they had done afterwards. I wasn't bothered, in fact I was glad that I wasn't going to have any more children, because I suffered so much with my husband.

Working in the USA
I came to the United States in 1971 for economic reasons. I wasn't interested in politics, only in working and being able to give my kids everything they needed. I had been separated from my husband for three years and was working in a factory from 7 o'clock in the morning until 10 o'clock at night, and still I wasn't earning enough. Coming here was the only way.

I left my children to look after themselves. My eldest daughter was 16 or 17. 'You go on, Mama', she told me. 'I'll look after them. I'll be able to help them with their studies because you will be supporting us.'

As my children say, in Guatemala everybody talks about how the United States is this and the United States is that. But coming here is hell. When I arrived I didn't know anybody and I didn't speak the language. Can you imagine? On the journey here I met some acquaintances from Guatemala. They were very good to me but I only stayed with them for about a week. I arrived on a Thursday and on the Monday I went to work as a domestic and was shut up in the house seven days a week. For years I looked after an old man whose son was a doctor. When he died he left me very good references, so I've never lacked for work. At one point I worked for a doctor who had a month-old baby. When the baby began talking the first word he said was my name. The mother cried and cried, and her husband told me to forgive her, it was because she was jealous.

There is so much discrimination here. If you don't speak perfect English they don't take any notice of you. If you want to be happy and get by in this country the only thing to do is act dumb. Hypocrisy is so common here. Your employers tell you how fond they are of you and how much they need you, but it's all lies. All lies. While you are doing what they want everything is fine, but as soon as you step the tiniest bit out of line you realise that there is no love. It's all hypocrisy.

In Guatemala, no matter how poor people are they'll always heat up a *tortilla* and a few beans and invite you to sit at their table and eat. Here in the States we Latins don't do that. We are just like everybody else, always working, striving... I've helped a lot of people who have come here, but as soon as their situation improves they move on without even asking how much they owe for the rent.

I would like to go back to Guatemala one day. You get homesick for your country. I have been here so long and I've worked so hard; I've given my best years to the United States. All my children are married now and have done well, two are psychologists. But people tell me that it is difficult to adapt; that if I go back I will have problems. The truth is you earn more here.

The real problem is that I didn't enter the United States legally. I blame the US Consulate in Guatemala. They kept telling me to come back the next month ... I waited two years, always hoping and changing from one job to another, because I was sure that they would give me a visa. Then one day someone at the consulate told me, 'Look, don't waste your time on this. I know an office where they can fix you up.' When I went to this office they told me not to worry, that I should just get a Mexican visa, and then when I was in Mexico I could get one for the United States. If they'd told me how I would have to cross the border I wouldn't have come, because it was very risky... But three years ago I went to Immigration and they are reviewing my case. I expect that one of these days they will call me and tell me that I have to leave the country.

I have heard that there are problems in Guatemala these days. I see it on the television and hear about it from people who say that

27

they have come here because of the situation. My family has never said anything about these problems. I don't know if it's because they don't want to upset me or because they are not aware of it. They tell me that there are problems in the countryside, but that they never hear or see anything.

I'm strong. I work hard and I want to do more. Otherwise I'd be saying, 'I'm tired, my children are grown up and have done well for themselves. They could support me now, so I'll leave.' But I am not going to do that. I'm independent and I do what I want. In that sense I am happy. I am free to do what I want.

The union makes us strong

An increasing number of Guatemalan women are finding employment in the nation's garment industry. Government statistics show that in 1980 approximately 12,000 women were employed in this sector. Today's figure is estimated to be at least double that. These clothing factories, which are frequently little more than sweatshops, are often owned by foreigners attracted by Guatemala's low labour costs. Attempts to organise trade unions in these establishments have met with considerable resistance from the owners. Between 1980 and 1986 some 103 trade union organisers were murdered.

Maria de los Angeles is a 39-year-old *ladina* woman who started work as a seamstress in a factory as an alternative to domestic service, which she found 'humiliating and morale destroying'. She married when she was 17; although the marriage broke up a month later she continued to see her ex-husband from time to time and has had four children by him. She now supports her three younger children alone, living with them in a single room in a poor suburb of Guatemala city. A key figure in the formation of a union at her workplace, in 1987 she led an all-woman factory occupation that lasted for three weeks.

I started work as a seamstress in a factory that makes children's clothes. The owner wanted me to be a kind of supervisor, but I didn't want to, because my workmates reacted badly. Then they fired some people, including me, and someone recommended I try another factory owned by Asians, where I earn 96 *quetzales* a month after social security payments are deducted.

At the factory our Asian employers treat us really badly. One of their wives even slapped an employee in the face. We have a supervisor who shouts extremely embarrassing things at us, especially as there are men around — personal insults. It was because of this that the idea of organising ourselves came about. Three of us visited another factory where the workers put us in contact with an umbrella organisation of Guatemalan trade unions, and we formed our union. It's just over a year now since we got organised and our struggle began. I've taken part right from the beginning, in all the decisions and everything.

It's the first time I've belonged to a union, and I love it. Since I joined, I've had to put up with my mother saying, 'You're going to end up dead. What about your children — you're a woman on her own'. But I've stood up to it, to everything they've said. My father is the only one who doesn't complain — he just tells me to be careful. I know that my mother is right; I *am* on my own and my work supports my kids. If I'm not there, my children will be on their own, because a grandmother is not the same as a mother. I understand my mother's point of view only too well. But I'm involved in the struggle because I hope that some day in the future when my kids, or one of my relatives, has to look for work, they won't have to suffer like I have at this factory.

Last year we decided to take over the factory. We did it because the management refused to negotiate with us. We found out that 150 of the workers were going to be fired. I was top of the list. At that time, the factory was in an ongoing dispute so they had no right to fire anyone. In a dispute the judge sets a deadline and during that period workers cannot be hired or fired without the judge's permission. However, they ignored this, we don't know how, and fired us.

So the factory was in dispute and we decided to occupy it to make ourselves heard. We knew it was the only way we could make the owners listen to us. The occupation only lasted a day, as our lawyer started to get things moving immediately. A new date was set, which meant that we could not be fired, so we went back to work.

From that day on the management began to separate us from the rest of the plant. We were put into a kind of alleyway behind the factory, which we called 'the chicken coop' because it really wasn't suitable for 65 people to work in. We were totally isolated from the factory and were only allowed access to it to go to the bathroom, or on those rare occasions when we had to go to the office. They even made us leave by another door. The supervisor told our other workmates not to associate with us because we unionists had leprosy and they could catch it! The management put a lot of ideas into their heads, mainly that if something should happen to their families it would be the union's fault...They also made them all sign a blank sheet of paper on which anything could be written later.

They kept the blinds down in the place where we worked and we had to sew by artificial light, which affected the eyesight of many of us. We were shut up in the heat and a foul smelling waste pipe overflowed around our feet. There was no ventilation whatsoever; it was like a cauldron. When we couldn't bear it any more, we soaked our clothes. They would dry within two or three minutes, so you can imagine how hot it was.

After that, when we had presented the owners with a collective contract and they had refused to negotiate with us, all the legal means were exhausted. We decided that they had to be made to listen to us one way or another, so we decided to occupy the factory.

The management thought that all the workers who supported us were taking part in the occupation, but in fact we were on our own. There were only us five from the union plus four from the advisory committee. A lot of our workmates arrived in the mornings to give us support, but that was during the day. At night we were by ourselves. We weren't afraid, however, because the other trade unions had people outside in the street. There was also a police patrol car. We knew we were being protected. Some other trade unions also brought us food: Cavisa brought sugar, Kerns brought Coca-Cola, and others gave us financial support. That's how we survived.

But I tell you, even though we sometimes felt happy, we were depressed because we couldn't be with our children — despite the fact that we knew we were struggling for something that would bear fruit later on. We put up with the sacrifice because we knew that afterwards we would be alright. So when we felt sad, we never let on to our workmates. We were always happy and enthusiastic in front of them and we'd try to find ways of cheering them up.

And so the days went by until it was 10 May, Mother's Day. Well, for me that 10 May was the saddest day of my life. It was the first Mother's Day that I hadn't been with my children. The students from the University of San Carlos came to cheer us up in the evening. They sang songs and wished us a happy Mother's Day. Even so, I felt really bad about my daughters — more so because my mother had come to see me and said, 'God wants you to settle this tomorrow. You decide: your daughters, or the factory and the cemetery.'

31

It was the hardest thing she could have said to me because I hadn't seen my daughters in the entire three weeks and two days that I'd been there. I didn't want them to come to the factory because I knew that it would upset them and that I would feel worse still because I couldn't leave. They called me on the phone, and I cried, but they couldn't see me.

I felt really dreadful that day because my mother also told me that my grandmother was seriously ill and might not last the night. I had to try and pull myself together because we had to go to court the next day.

We left the factory the morning of 11 May to go to the court, where we stayed until 3 o'clock, when we went to the union headquarters, getting back to the factory at about 5 o'clock. As soon as we got there they told me that my daughter had just called and that my grandmother had died. I asked for permission to go to the wake, but I couldn't go to the funeral because we had a general meeting that day.

The next day our lawyer told us to hand over the keys to the owners because the Vice-President of Guatemala had intervened. The owners had agreed to negotiate with us and no one was to be fired. So the keys were handed over to them although, in fact, the factory had been open the whole time. It was just that they had been afraid to enter. They arrived to count their merchandise. It was all exactly as they had left it because we hadn't touched a thing.

For us, those days and the takeover of the factory remain the event of our lives, something wonderful that we will never experience again — something we've been told we should write about, so that in the future others can say, 'If they did it, why can't we?' Everybody congratulated us because, as they said, 'In spite of being women you put up a good fight.' We knew that everyone was counting on us.

This struggle has given us women friendship and support. We have tried to find a way to be united because, as you know, 'The people united will never be defeated'. It's a cliché, but nevertheless very true. We all trust each other equally. There's none of this, 'I prefer her, or her.' We are very close.

In terms of my hopes for Guatemala, the best and most wonderful thing would be if all of us women had a job. It's fundamental. We should all have a job with dignity, where we could earn enough to be able to provide for our kids... And then, that there be peace here in Guatemala. That's what we most desire: peace. If all the disappearances and reprisals should come to an end it would be the most beautiful thing in the world.

2
BEING INDIAN

Making progress

Government figures show that over half of all Guatemalans live in abject poverty and are unable to afford even a basic diet. Vitalina is a *Quiché* Indian in her 30s who works for a local development agency. She has managed to break away from her expected role in an environment of misery and ignorance to do work that she enjoys, and which is beneficial to her community. To achieve this she has had to make certain sacrifices, including denying herself a partner and children. This, in turn, has made her an anomaly, creating problems of acceptance for her in the very communities that she strives to help.

I am from a very poor family. I had 12 brothers and sisters, but we were so poor that eight died. One brother was killed in the recent violence, but all the others died of malnutrition when they were very little.

My father was a pedlar and my mother is a weaver. She was able to help the family a lot with her weaving. But my parents were never able to give us enough to eat, and I've been sickly since I was a child. They could never take us to a doctor; my father said prayers for us and we had to get better that way. God must have wanted me to live.

I was able to go to school, though. I started when I was nine. It was difficult for me, but I managed to finish primary school. My other brothers and sisters didn't have the opportunity of going to school, as my parents hid them in the lanes around the house. Through a lack of awareness, they believed that their children didn't need education. They preferred us to start work from an early age, helping them. If you don't learn how to work the land, you won't know how to cultivate it properly and there'll be no harvest.

When I was about ten or twelve I started thinking about what I was going to do. I never thought of getting married and getting someone to support me, I wanted to earn my own living. My mother is the same, and she has given me a lot of support. I decided to go on with my schooling so that one day I could earn enough to clothe myself and help my parents. I thought it would be better to study. So I didn't fall in love because then I would have got married.

When I finished primary school I came to town and went to the convent, where I translated for the nuns from *Quiché* to Spanish — we only spoke *Quiché* at home but at school I had learnt some Spanish. I worked there as a volunteer, only one Thursday and Saturday every month.

Then one of the nuns became interested in my situation. She suggested that maybe I had a vocation to be a nun and that I should become a boarder at the nun's school. I told my parents, but they said there was no money to send me to the school. I felt so bad. I spent entire nights thinking about it. I decided that I must go. The sister said that I would only have to pay three *quetzales*, so my mother struggled to get the money together. But I failed the final exam — I don't know what went wrong. I didn't feel at home there, and I couldn't stand being shut up like that. But I carried on anyway, and the next year I passed the course.

Then the time came when my family couldn't pay even the three *quetzales*, on top of which we were told we had to wear a uniform. The sister worked it so I didn't have to wear one, but I decided to leave anyway. I didn't have the heart for it, so I went home. But I started thinking, 'What am I doing? I can't give up just like that. I have to get back into it.' So I started all over again, but this time I went to an ordinary school, a national institute, and not as a boarder. In this way I passed my second and third basic courses.

After that I decided to carry on with my studies and to become a teacher. I had to work out how to do it, because my parents didn't have enough money to help us with studying. My mother was still doing her weaving, but my father had become ill and couldn't work. He had rheumatism, he drank a lot early on, so maybe that was why. So I decided to get a job. I started to work in my old primary school and worked there for six months. I made snacks for the 300 children and lunch for the nine teachers. They paid me 35 *quetzales* a month, most of which I saved towards my studies. I made a couple of *trajes*, bought myself a pair of shoes to wear to the institute and helped my father out when he was a bit short on cash. January came, and I enrolled at the Juan de Leon Institute.

In the fourth form, my health deteriorated because I was eating very irregularly and I had to travel a long way every day as I couldn't afford a room in town. I had gastritis very badly and malaria, and problems with my liver. I thought I was going to die. It was only when they took me to Guatemala City that I was cured.

In 1980 I returned to the institute but came to live in town because it was too far for me to travel every day. In order to save money I cooked over a coal fire. All the money I'd saved, and more, had been spent on getting cured from my illness. So I had to start weaving.

Since I was small I've been interested in weaving. My mother made *huipiles* and sold them to the tourists. That's how she managed to feed us. I adore weaving — it's my art. When I was in fifth form my schoolmates asked me to weave something for the wall, so I made a small weaving with '10 May, Mothers' Day' woven into it. They liked it and asked me to make more. In this way I earned five *quetzales* a week which was enough for me to live on. I managed to put myself through fifth and sixth form solely on what I earned from my weavings.

I've been very creative. My mother only taught me how to start out, how to make the patterns. But as she was illiterate she didn't show me how to make the written designs — I invented them myself. So I designed the letters and through that I was able to sell things. Necessity forces you to look for ways of selling things.

All *huipiles* are different. Some are in the old designs; not just anybody can make them. There are very few women who still know how to. The majority copy cross-stitch designs of flowers and birds from Mexican magazines.

When I started weaving, I never thought that I would be able to work at it full time. It's a miracle that I got the job that I have today at the Association. One day my brother came running to tell me that a woman I had met in town was looking for me, and I was to go and see her right away at the cooperative. When I got there they asked me if I would like to work with a group of women in Santa Rosa, and if 150 *quetzales* salary was alright. I told them I had no experience in how to charge for work, but that it was fine — better than earning nothing!

At the moment I am in charge of a small artisan project, and teach handicrafts to women in an emergency programme that the Association runs. When everything was very bad in 1980 and 1981, people in some communities weren't able to sow corn. When we arrived they had no maize — all they could do was plait palm fronds to sell to make hats. Nearly all of them were widows, and no one was helping them out. Their children were malnourished, some with grade three malnutrition. Their stomachs were swollen and their hair had gone blonde. In one hamlet alone there were 75 widows. They told us that many men were killed one afternoon, when the army arrived and took the men out of the houses. They killed them right there, men and boys. They took the bodies away in a lorry, who knows where.

To begin with, the Association's programme supplied this community with food, because the people had nothing. Then they told the people that they would have to work in order to support themselves. I stayed in their hamlet with them to teach the women handicrafts, whatever they wanted to learn. It's a depressing place, not like a big village. But I quickly got used to the people, and felt good being with them.

The women I work with always ask me why I'm not married and don't have children. Sometimes they say I am 'bad'. But it doesn't bother me. I am what I am, and I defend my point of view. I don't want to get married — I prefer to be left in peace. Also, I'm the one supporting my parents these days. The main reason I've never got married is because most women in rural areas are not allowed to leave the house when they want to. Their husbands get jealous, or they have to look after the children. In my case, if I can't leave my work because I'm very busy, nobody will nag me. That doesn't mean that because I am on my own I'm going to be out all hours, but, if there is a lot of work I don't like to leave it half done.

Right now a lot of changes are taking place. Many, many people from communities like the one where I was born are coming to town to study. It's a sign that they see what progress they can make, so they struggle and struggle to get ahead. What has given me most satisfaction is that I have managed to do something that is of benefit to my family and my people.

A widow's story

The silence that envelops Guatemala's remote Indian villages is one of the first things that impresses outsiders, particularly city dwellers. María's tiny village, situated many miles up a dirt road in the Cuchumatan mountains in the west of the country, has no electricity, telephone, radio, or other means of communicating with the outside world. Its gentle, agrarian beauty is wrapped in a total silence in which every sound reverberates like a bell. That silence was shattered one midday during 1981 when the Guatemalan army arrived in María's village. Now most of the women there are widows.

The villagers are still acutely afraid, but Indians from the same indigenous group, working with a local development organisation, have helped them to restore their lives by providing supplies, ideas and practical help. In many ways conditions in the village have improved. María, a *Quiché* Indian in her 40s who never went to school and who speaks only broken Spanish, points to the widows' rabbit breeding project. The rabbits are a new and important source of protein for the families. The widows have also learned to look after their animals and tend to their small plots of land, tasks formerly carried out by their husbands. They now grow vegetables, some of which they sell for money to buy clothes and school materials for their children. Previously they earned only a pittance through the tedious plaiting of straw for panama hats. They are also being taught the intricate kind of weaving needed to make the traditional Indian *huipil*.

While the women undoubtedly find this work an added burden, they take pride in what they have accomplished and possess a new self-confidence. They have formed new relationships, learned to express their opinions and to make important decisions. Previously they related to the world primarily through their husbands. Yet there is one aspect of their widowhood that is still neglected, and that is emotional support to help them cope with their bereavement. María, outwardly one of the strongest and most confident of the widows, wept throughout this interview. It was one of the few occasions when she had had the opportunity to talk openly about her husband's death.

My name is María. I am 44 years old. I was born here in this village. I have had 16 children: 11 are still alive, five are dead. I am a widow now. When the 'sickness' happened they killed my husband ... By the 'sickness' I mean the violence.

Patrols of soldiers came to kill the people here, and I lost my husband. But I didn't leave — why should I? What crime was I committing? If they were going to kill us, they would kill us. They had weapons and they frightened my children and me. But I wasn't going to leave.

My husband is dead. I wish it had been through illness because I know what that is. God tells us that we are all going to die. We know that we will die when the time comes. But to kill you by surprise like that! If my husband had been ill then I could have tried to find a cure or something, and if it hadn't worked then it would have been God's will. But to be tortured and killed like that ... that's what hurts me the most.

When my husband was alive, I didn't go to work. I have too many kids. I looked after the house, cooked the meals, did the washing. Now it's all changed. Since he was killed, I've started working on our corn patch and looking after the animals. I get up at 5.30am every morning. I do some chores and at about 6.30am I make the breakfast. We have coffee and *tortillas* and beans. If there is a bit of cheese or some eggs we have that as well. Then I take my cow and two goats to pasture. I have pigs and hens too. At 11.30am I come back to the house to prepare the midday meal. In the afternoon, I take the animals to feed again. And I have to collect the firewood as well! I have two jobs, but what else can I do? I have no husband, nothing, just the children ...

I am a midwife and sometimes there are women to see to. I have attended 75 births in this community. A health clinic is going to be opened soon near here, and then I will be able to get prescriptions and take them to the chemist. At the moment I use oils and camomile tea...

Now that my children are growing up I need my husband, to talk about when the corn will be ready for picking, what work needs to be done next, what to do about the house, the kids, how to cure them when they are sick. Nowadays I have to make these decisions on my own. I've never considered getting married again because of the kids. What would I do with them? No man would want them: it's too much expense. It's better that I stay with my kids. My friends are widows too, and they have to struggle to bring their kids up. We help each other, we take turns at doing things.

To begin with, we didn't know what to do. We didn't have enough money to buy corn or feed our children. Then we heard that the Association was helping people in another village, so I and my sister-in-law, also a widow, went to talk to them. They told us to get together with other women in the same situation. And so we got started. First, Vitalina came and taught us how to plait straw; later we are going to make baskets. Then José came along — he is going to teach us how to grow vegetables, and they will give us the seeds. I am going to plant onions and sugar beet, and I will sell them in the market. I'll have money and I'll be able to feed my children.

What I want is to be able to go on working, and for my children to grow up and help me out, because life is very hard here.

Away from home

The savagery that took place in the Guatemalan highlands in the early 1980s is estimated to have displaced about one million people, mainly Indians. Many headed for Guatemala City, where they tried to find cover in the marginal life of the slum areas surrounding the capital. Urban life forces them to abandon many of their customs and, particularly painful for Mayan Indians, it breaks their sacred ties to the cultivation of land. Often they are unable even to wear their traditional clothing, for fear of being identified as coming from 'troublesome' villages. Many Indian women have not been able to resist the impact of *ladino* culture on their lives and have drifted into alcoholism, prostitution and other practices unacceptable in their rural communities.

Victoria, an *Achi* Indian from Baja Verapaz, has fought against any such deterioration of her traditional values and customs. She still wears her *traje* and armours herself with a deep disdain for most things *ladino*. A 27-year-old primary school teacher, she lives with her husband in a small room in a squatter settlement on the periphery of Guatemala City. Many of her ideas on women's issues appear very conservative, but they should be understood in the context of her intense desire to preserve her culture and identity. The fear she lives under and her yearning for the countryside became obvious when she insisted on being interviewed outdoors, because 'only the trees will overhear us'.

My village is so wonderful, you can't imagine ... to me it is such a special place. It's where I spent my childhood, and I left part of my life there. I have good memories of it, but also very bad ones because it was there that my two brothers disappeared.

Today there are many problems, many *orejas* or informers [literally 'ears']. The military commander who is responsible for so many deaths still lives there. These are the negative things that prevent us from going back. But it's where our land is, our home — everything. Our house has been ransacked, there is nothing left. The heads of the civil defense patrols divided everything up between them and took over our land as well. It's been one problem after another since my brothers disappeared.

My younger brother was 17 years old and the older was 25 when they disappeared in 1981. My mother had just given birth to my youngest brother, and one of my other brothers had tried to register the birth. But the authorities paid no attention to him because he was only 15. My father had had to leave the village earlier because of the violence — the army was after him — and I was a boarder at the convent in the city. I was the only one my father trusted and who knew where he was. Nobody else knew, not even my mother. I was responsible for dealing with any problems that arose at home. So my father sent for me to register the birth, as it's supposed to be done within 15 days.

I went to see my brother, a seminarian, to tell him I was going to the village. He hadn't been back for three years and was feeling homesick; he wanted to go with me. Then my other brother who was working as a mechanic decided to go as well. He was the one who was closest to my mother — he really loved her. My father warned them that it was really dangerous there as the army was arresting everybody. But they paid no attention and we left one Saturday. On the Sunday, we couldn't do anything because everything was closed, but on the Monday, I went to the town hall to see the mayor and try to sort out the problem. I realised something was wrong by the way his secretary answered me: 'I don't have to cry over other people's problems', he said. 'I can pay you if you do this for me', I said. 'I only want to register the birth because it's been a month now and they will fine us. That's what I want to avoid.' He said, 'But today is a holiday.' 'I'll pay you', I said. And I gave him 15 *quetzales*. He told me to leave the details and to come back at two o'clock, when the birth certificate would be ready.

It was then about 12 o'clock so we went to have lunch. We were really enjoying ourselves because we were all together, my mother, my brothers, the baby and me — all reunited. Then the priest came out and said to us, 'Be careful, things aren't going well around here. Be on your guard.' 'But father, if we haven't done anything, what have we to fear?' said my brother, who had done his military service and had been discharged just a month earlier. 'My papers are in order', he said. 'Yes', said the priest, 'but since you have left the army you have no legal protection'. 'Don't worry', my brother replied, 'we are leaving right away, anyway'. Since it was already two o'clock we decided that the two men would go to the town hall while I took my mother to the dispensary. We agreed to meet again at three o'clock.

We have never seen my brothers since. We have no idea what happened, where they went, or where they were taken. We have no idea if they are alive or dead. The most likely thing is that they are dead, because it's been over five years now.

We are afraid to go back to the village now. We have no guarantees. Of course we would like to, because nobody lives contentedly where they were not born, where they don't cultivate the land. Everything that belongs to us is there. But if we went back it would be nothing more than handing ourselves over to the army. It's difficult living here in the capital, very difficult...

The importance of being Indian

Although I live in the capital, I still speak my native language. We don't speak Spanish at home because it's not our language, and my husband is Indian from the same ethnic group as me. When I was born, my father and my grandfather made a pact. My grandfather wanted to preserve our Indian traditions for ever, so he asked my father to promise that we wouldn't alter our customs or our culture. Even if someone tried to force me to change my *traje* for *ladino* clothes on pain of death I wouldn't do so.

I first met *ladinos* when I was seven, when I tried to enrol in primary school. I received a rebuff at the time that I've never forgotten. The teacher was a *ladina* and by chance I was the last child to enrol, but they wouldn't let me because there were no desks left. My father went to see the teacher and begged her to let me stay in the class. She refused and said, 'She's just one more Indian who wants an education.'

This was to affect me a lot, not at the time because I was too young to understand her contempt, but later on. My father, however, understood all too well, and it was thanks to this teacher's disdain that another little school came about. It was built by my father, who was then president of the village council, and his three brothers, with materials provided by the community. So, as a result of this teacher's scorn, 60 more children from the community were able to go to school the following year...

According to *ladinos*, we Indians have no God. I thought it was very strange once when I heard a priest say that for Indians, Christ

45

had never been born. I thought very deeply about this. Did this mean to say that my people were just savages, that they had no God? I couldn't accept this because I had seen how my grandmother carried out animal sacrifices, how she worshipped St. Anthony of the Mountain who was her saint of animals and the land. We Indians are 100 per cent religious, we believe in divine works. According to the historians, the Mayans were polytheistic. They believed in the God of the Rain, the God of the Sun, the God of the Moon. But this isn't true polytheism. Indians have only one God, it is just that we identify him with different aspects of nature.

There are two kinds of Indian: true Indians and those who are Indian in terms of blood and nationality, but who want to be better than others, so start to use things that are inappropriate to us. There are Indians, for example, who say that it is bad for you to have a lot of children, so they take contraceptives. The true Indian doesn't use contraceptives. We accept children as they come.

These days, there are also Indian women who use their bodies commercially, like the Rabina Hau [the winner of a beauty-queen contest for Indian women], who makes an exhibition of herself for a few dollars. In other words, not all Indians value our culture. There are many of us who for a title or a job stop being what we are.

I'm careful not to put a foot wrong because there are many eyes on me: not just my husband or my family, but also members of my community. I feel part of this community, and I don't want to let people down.

Looking to the future

I have no hope in *ladinos*. I have no hope because it would be very difficult to civilise the *ladino* into our way of thinking. It is difficult for us to understand each other. I put my hopes, my faith and my trust in those of my Indian people who are fighting for change.

I view the future very negatively, because this generation is one without hope. Some of our culture, however, *is* being preserved through the revolutionary organisations. There are not many of them, but they are what helps us to carry on.

There are attempts to unite poor *ladinos* and Indians in revolutionary action because poor *ladinos* are also manipulated. These are *ladinos* who are aware of their own misfortune and are seeking a solution. They find hope in the struggle. We cannot reject them because, in spite of all the harm they have done us, we Indians are very forgiving.

Yet many Indians will not forgive — quite the opposite. There is a lot of hatred as a result of all the violence. I know that it's not good to hate, but the only thing the Indian has left now is revenge. I believe that the sons and daughters of those who fell are planning to avenge their parents' death when they grow up. I think that they will do it, because it's not just one, or two, or three, but thousands and thousands that have been left orphans. Thousands of women that have been widowed and thousands of 13-year-old girls that have been raped. And the children of these killers, born as a result of these rapes, have hatred and revenge mixed in their blood. I believe that in ten to 15 years these children will become revolutionaries.

Racism

A 40-year-old *ladina* journalist talks about the common *ladina* view of Indians.

I believe that one of the reasons why the repression did not cause too big a commotion among Guatemalans in the capital was because it was mainly Indians that were affected. All the suffering that took place was not *really* suffering because it happened to Indians. The Guatemalan upper class believes that Indians cannot really feel, that an Indian woman will not truly suffer if her husband or children are killed because she is not 'the same as us'. They say, 'Well, they were Indians weren't they?'

One of the things that most shocks foreigners is that people in the capital were unaware of what went on. I was once invited to lunch by a woman who asked me if it was true that there were war orphans. Another upper class woman asked me if Indians ever laughed.

There are really two societies in Guatemala, *ladino* and indigenous, and I don't think that they are ever going to become one because neither is interested in achieving this. Politicians pay lip service to the idea, because the Indians represent five million votes. But that is their only value — votes.

Being Indian in Guatemala City

Every Sunday, the rather forlorn and slightly tarnished central plaza of Guatemala City takes on the lively air of a colourful Indian market-place. On this, their one day off a week, hundreds of young Indian women wearing their native costumes take over the square. They chat and laugh with their friends, flirt, eat candy floss and roasted corn, and pose for photographs in front of the pale-green National Palace, the scene of countless coups and counter-coups.

The women making the most of this day of freedom work as domestic servants — the occupation of more than one-third of all women wage-earners in Guatemala. The majority are Indians of *campesina* origin and are usually employed as live-in maids, an arrangement which works out cheaper for their employers. Their work is tedious, tiring and demeaning. But for most of these women, coming to work in the capital is the only alternative to a life of extreme poverty in their villages. It can, for example, mean that they manage to get a minimum of education, they will probably learn some Spanish, and they will make a little money. They will, however, be in daily contact with a level of racial discrimination that does not exist to the same extent, if at all, in their home village. Working in the capital also often hastens the process of acculturation, whereby ultimately the women do not feel at home either in their own or *ladino* culture.

Margarita is a 24-year-old *Cakchiquel* Indian from Patzun, who works as a live-in servant and believes that she has found a place for herself between Guatemala's two cultures.

I came to the capital to work when I was eight years old, as my parents are very poor and they weren't able to support us all. There are seven of us, and they couldn't send us to school. Since we were very little we've had to look out for ourselves as best we could.

I came to Guatemala City and worked with a family in Zone II. I started when I was eight and left when I was 18... The first thing the *señora* [lady of the house] did was to teach me housework. I had

49

to do the shopping, the cleaning and wash the dishes. I worked in the mornings and in the afternoon I would go to school for a few hours. The family was fond of me, but they were very strict about everything, very demanding. I was supposed not to think too much, just to do things as fast as possible. I would often have to get up at around 3 or 4 o'clock in the morning because of the water shortages. There was usually only water at that time of the day, and I had to fill all the buckets. It was really hard because I normally had to work until 9 or 10 o'clock at night — virtually the only thing I thought about was work. When I was about 12 years old, I stopped going to school because there was no time. I was so tired that I couldn't apply my mind to studying. I went back to it later, in the evenings, but I never really had the time.

I don't mind cleaning, cooking and working in the kitchen. What I don't like is people who exploit you. When I was growing up there was a lot of that in my life. Sometimes the people I first worked for beat me and treated me badly. At times I would answer back and they would punish me. 'Your parents didn't bring you up, we did,' they said, 'and you have to obey us if you want to stay here. If you don't, then find somewhere else to go.' They know that you need the work — the money — and they try to make you suffer even more than you're already suffering.

It's really only now that I am meeting other people that I realise the difference between people here and people in my village. I don't want to speak badly of the people in the capital, but I've suffered this treatment in the flesh — the disdain that always exists because you are Indian. They think they have to crush you because you work for them. For example, I had to eat first, then the family ate; if I ate off a plate then it mustn't be touched; these plates were theirs and this plate was mine — everything was kept separate.

In the beginning, I really missed my family. It was very difficult to adjust to life here in Guatemala City. But the family I worked for had a little girl and she really loved me. We played together and as time passed I forgot nearly everything about my life in the village. The little girl was a *ladina*, obviously, and we were always treated differently. Her mother used to tell her that I was different. Later she got married and I went to work in her house. But she married into a family with a lot of money and she became more demanding, more arrogant. She began to treat me differently. It was money that made her change. I hardly ever see her now. But I still think of her family as my second parents — they were the ones who gave me some education, after all.

A conflict of customs

Nearly every Sunday I go to my village to see my parents. I love my family, my people and my village, and I've always loved going there. I like their traditions and customs. But I grew up in another environment, I didn't grow up in the countryside, cultivating the land. If you asked me how I would feel if I went back there permanently, I would have to say that I wouldn't be happy, because I am used to things here in the city.

Very few village people really know the capital. They are very poor, and there are few possibilities for them to come here. Many of them view coming here in a negative light. They say that if you come here to live, you are a lost cause. I think that's true, especially if you don't know how to run your life, because here in Guatemala City there are many ways of life, good and bad. You have to have a lot of self-control. In the village, they see how people change after coming here. How they don't want to wear their *trajes*. They are always asking me, 'What do you do in the city? What kind of work do you have? How do people treat you?' They are very simple people, and even when you explain they still don't understand, because they have nothing with which to compare it.

The life of an Indian woman in the countryside is to work the land, collect firewood, carry water, wash the clothes in the river and take the animals to pasture. I haven't done any of this. The only tradition I retain is wearing my *traje* and speaking my native language. I like to wear my *traje*, and I think I ought to, since all my family still wears it. When I was growing up I wore a dress, but when I was 15 the family I worked for told me I should try wearing my *traje*. The husband's parents were indigenous, and he thought that I shouldn't abandon my customs. 'You should do what your people do', he told me. 'They all wear *traje* and it is very beautiful.' It was a big thing for me to start wearing it.

Indian customs demand that we marry our own people. It isn't that we don't like *ladinos*, but it would be a problem for us. I should marry an Indian from my village, or a village nearby. Most importantly he should be from the same indigenous group, *Cakchiquel*. In fact, my boyfriend is from my village, but he is studying in the city to be an engineer. He would like us to get

51

married and live here, going back to our village every week or so to see our families. In other words, he no longer wants to adjust to life in the village. It would be very difficult for people like us to adapt to the customs of the village indigenous people.

Men like him, who have been educated and have more experience, tend to have relationships with women like me who are able to speak Spanish well. It doesn't matter what you do, if you are a teacher or a nurse, or whatever. He says, 'I like it because you are sure of yourself in your relationships with other people. I wouldn't like to have someone who never talked, who couldn't relate to my friends.' So marrying someone who has never left the village would be very difficult. They wouldn't know what it is to have a house, to have things like an electric stove or a television, though many Indians nowadays would like the chance. Our intention is to take the good things from the *ladino* way of life.

Prejudice

A 50-year-old *ladina* government worker talks about racist attitudes to the Indian majority.

Like all Guatemalans, I grew up with prejudices towards the indigenous population. I am of mixed blood, but still I discriminated against Indians. When I was a child, I didn't like to sit next to an Indian at school, because I believed that they were dirty and had lice. It wasn't until I went to study at university in Guatemala City that I felt uneasy about the situation of the indigenous population. Up until then, the relationship I had had with Indian women was one of domination. They were domestic workers and I was their employer, or they would sell me things in the market. I was always in a superior position: I could buy or not, or I could bargain and get the Indian woman to sell it to me cheaper.

The problem of racism permeates the whole population here, not only whites, and not only the upper classes. Amongst the poor *ladinos* there is also discrimination towards the Indians who are poor. In other words, virtually no social class or stratum is free from it.

Defining cultural identity

The National Women's Office (Onam) was created by the military dictatorship that ruled Guatemala in 1980. It remained largely non-operational, however, until a civilian government took office in 1986 and a woman was appointed Minister of Labour. Under the auspices of the Labour Ministry, Onam's budget was increased and a new director was appointed. The stated aim of the office is 'to promote and help women', primarily through education and development projects. Onam has a small library of information on Guatemalan women, as well as a publication, *Nosotras*, the content of which reflects the office's rather bureaucratic and non-feminist orientation.

Gloria, a 35-year-old Indian woman and director of Onam, has a degree in sociology and comes from a middle-class family in the process of acculturation. Although she is bilingual in Spanish and her native *Pocomchí* language, she identifies herself as wholly Indian.

I belong to the Pocomchí indigenous group, from the north of Guatemala. It's a relatively small, but very traditional group. I feel very content because it has defined my cultural identity for me.

In Guatemala it is very important to be clear about the differences between the indigenous and non-indigenous woman. Indian women, being Indian, the Indian entity is a mentality rooted in our culture. The non-Indian does not have these cultural roots. As an Indian woman I would say that we are in a much better position because we deeply respect the family hierarchy and our community organisation. We are part of an order that has roots, we have our own language and we have a solid cultural identity in spite of there having been a lot of acculturation. We have a rich religion with a cosmological content, and it is very easy for us to decide to struggle for someone else...

Up to now, I would say that the indigenous woman's overriding problem has been economic: there is enormous, chronic poverty. And if there are no resources there can be no development. The

Indian woman is ready to work at the drop of a hat, but she lacks opportunities. Furthermore, we have a health problem. People criticise the Indian woman for being very traditionalist, but institutionalised health programmes have not reached where they should, so women are forced to use natural medicine. The health service is not fulfilling its role. Midwives, for example, provide part of the medical service, but they don't know how to undertake surgery. They could, but they haven't been trained adequately. There's a lack of health education in Guatemala.

Then there is malnutrition. How is this overburdened Indian woman going to feed her family? Where is she going to get the food from? And hygiene... you might want to teach better hygiene, but there's no clean water available. You teach people that they should change their clothes two or three times a week, but how can they change their clothes if they don't have any clean clothes to change into? The development ideal must face up to reality.

I'd say that the woman bears the brunt. She's the one who has the children, who has to prepare the food, support the family, wash the clothes. You should take into account that there are a large number of widows, very young widows, who have to act as both mother and father and support not just one or two, but often three or more kids.... All of this this is very detrimental to the Indian woman's health.

There is a clear contrast with the situation of the *ladina* woman. Usually she is in closer contact with the infrastructure, with development. In other words, she is more privileged. We should also consider that *ladina* women are in a minority, and that they mostly live in urban areas. Indian families, on the other hand, usually live in rural areas and are often subject to forced migrations. They are uprooted and made to leave land that is theirs, but not in the eyes of the law. It's a very complex problem relating to the whole question of land tenure.

On top of that, there is an acute linguistic problem in Guatemala, where we have 29 indigenous languages. The authorities can't decide whether it is better to integrate the Indian into the Spanish language or to teach Indians in their own language. All of this has meant a serious setback in the development process, because in their determination to decide on one or other plan, all programmes have been delayed. Personally, I learnt Spanish as a maternal language, because my parents taught me both languages. I think it gives you an advantage up to a certain point. But it is a very questionable issue because of the racist attitude prevailing in all levels of society. Also, language is often confused with nationality in our country.

Illiteracy is another thing. You can arrive in a community and teach 40, 50 or 100 people to read and write, but they'll become illiterate again because they have no use for it. There is no ongoing education. In other words, the education provided is dysfunctional to our needs. It should be regionalised, by generating human resources to teach every type of community in every corner of the country in their own language. Spanish could also be taught because it is useful, but people shouldn't have one thing taken from them in order to be given another in half-measure, which is what happens at the moment. Teachers arrive at [rural] schools, they prevent people from speaking their native language and in exchange they provide a badly spoken, badly pronounced, and often badly taught Spanish. There is no continuity and in the end people don't speak either language well... If you are going to take away the indigenous language, at least provide people with one they can speak well.

In Guatemala, there is a lot of ignorance about Indians. For example, our *trajes*. For me, my *traje* is like a flag. It is the identity of my people. It is not mine, not Gloria's nor my brother's or sisters' — rather it belongs to a whole people with deep historical roots. The simple act of wearing it identifies one, anywhere, anytime, at every social level. My *traje* contains so much, even mystical and spiritual value.

Indian love
There are many misconceptions about the indigenous couple. Many years ago, I met a psychologist who wanted to do a study on the sexual relations of Indian couples. I told her that I thought it presumptive on her part, because she could never give an objective opinion since she would have to be with a couple while they were being intimate. However, I can tell you that the father of my daughter is an Indian and I have had experiences with other Indians. Our emotional concepts, the whole of our emotional life, what is called our sexual life, have to be judged according to other values. Our values are what defines our behaviour. Let's say, for example, that for the *ladina* woman tenderness is expressed by the man embracing her in the street. For us, it would be just the opposite.

You cannot stereotype: we have our own ways of experiencing our emotional life. I don't agree with talking about the presence or absence of tenderness, as you have to be part of the couple. But I do know that there are other ways of showing emotion...

Of course, it should be pointed out that the man who is in the process of transculturation — such as an Indian man who is living in a marginalised area — will never behave like a man living in a strictly Indian environment. The Indian couple has very, very solid values because we respect our history. Proof of this is the extremely low incidence of divorce, prostitution, rape and infidelity that exists in Indian communities.

The *ladina* woman, on the other hand, suffers from feelings of passionate jealousy. The indigenous woman is very prudent, she knows what she wants and this makes the man less *macho*. But, of course, I must insist that it depends on the context... That's why among us Indians you cannot talk about feminism or *machismo* because we were brought up in this other context, where a woman knows that she has a commitment to her partner; she doesn't view it as an obligation, but rather as an equilibrium.

I didn't like the focus that Luz Méndez de la Vega [a Guatemalan feminist writer] gave in one newspaper article, when she said that one of our sacred books, the *Chilam Balam*, portrays the woman as a dog walking behind the man... The indigenous couple is one of the most integrated, because the Indian woman is very conscious of her role *vis-à-vis* the man, and the man fulfils his obligations.

When Luz Méndez talks about women's culture, she does so within the feminist/*macho* framework and this is not relevant to the Indian woman. It may even be that we will never, ever experience this stage. Luckily for us, we respond to another social and cultural context!

Machismo

A 25-year-old *Cakchiquel* Indian talks about attitudes towards men in various Indian communities.

Machismo takes on different forms in the various Indian communities. Some communities still accept the situation that has been forced on them for centuries, and this is reflected in how the woman walks behind the man and serves him food, among other things.

At home, we were always told that the man eats first and we eat last. The man can beat you as hard as he likes but you must have respect for him. In some communities the traditional ceremonies also centre on men. But there are other communities where the women, realising that the community needs them, venture out of their homes.

The attraction of evangelism

Hundreds of thousands of Guatemalans have joined evangelical sects in recent years. Part of the attraction of these sects is their emphasis on the 'life hereafter', which releases people from the burden and potential risk involved in taking action to improve their conditions here on earth.

Members of the sects have also been relatively protected from army repression, unlike members of the Catholic Church, which is viewed by the Guatemalan ultra-right as fundamentally subversive because of the prominent role it has played in encouraging people to stand up for their rights.

A further attraction, especially for women, is the sects' prohibition of alcohol. For many women, this has meant fewer beatings from alcoholic husbands and more money to spend on their families. Women also frequently play a more prominent role in these churches than they do in the Catholic Church, and Indian women in particular are freed from some of the more inhibiting traditions of their ethnic groups. Evangelism, however, can be a divisive element in traditional Indian communities. Members of the sects tend to acquire *ladino* habits in both behaviour and outlook, and the social organisation of indigenous life is destroyed.

Margarita, a young *Cakchiquel* Indian woman, is a member of an evangelical sect.

Religion is very important to us evangelicals. It's the number one thing. My parents had become evangelicals by the time I was born and I grew up an evangelical. I think it is very important to have a religion, to believe in God, to have faith: to have something to fill the vacuum within us.

There are many differences between us and Catholics. In the first place, if you are a Catholic you have to get baptised, have first communion, and be confirmed, and you have to worship a certain God. According to the Catholics in my village, the God there is St

Bernardino. We have to believe that he is *our* saint, of *our* village. There is a lot of worshipping of idols. This doesn't exist among evangelicals. Each of us can decide of our own free will, when we are older, whether we want to be baptised or not. We follow what is said in the Bible.

There are a lot of problems in the village because the Catholics are always fighting with the evangelicals. They say that we are crazy and that we don't know what we are doing, because we are always saying that God is coming and he never comes ... And they say that we are boring because our religion doesn't permit us to go to dances, to drink, or to wear the necklaces that are traditional among our people. The Catholic religion permits all of this — anything goes.

Exiled from my Quiché home

During the 1980s nearly a quarter of a million Guatemalans were forced to leave their country due to army violence. Most fled to Mexico, the nearest point of safety and attainable on foot. Virtually all the Guatemalan refugees in Mexico are Indian *campesinos*, and of an estimated refugee population of more than 100,000 only 43,000 live in official camps. The remainder fend for themselves as best they can, living among the local population and usually passing themselves off as Mexicans.

Only a small percentage of the refugees have accepted the Guatemalan government's offer to return to their country. A considerable percentage of these have run into problems on their return, such as discovering that their lands have been expropriated or that they are regarded with suspicion by the local military authorities. Some have been resettled in model villages, and nearly all have had to participate in the civil patrols.

Those who stay in Mexico face the challenge of trying to maintain their culture. When their children are born they become Mexican citizens and attend Mexican schools. However, probably because of their extremely strong ties to their ancient communities, most Guatemalan Indians appear to be making a decided effort to retain their language and customs.

Juana, a 23-year-old *Quiché* Indian, lives in a Mexican village not unlike the highland villages of Guatemala.

There are many more women than men among the Guatemalan refugees in Mexico. Most of them are women who have been widowed. I am a widow and so is my mother, so are the women in two of the other four Guatemalan families in this village. Three of my cousins are orphans and are living here with my grandparents.

I left Guatemala with my son in 1982. I was 17 years old and my son was a three-week-old baby. We were being persecuted because my parents were catechists, involved in Catholic Action, as were my brothers and sisters and my grandparents. My father had organised a large group of young people who participated in cultural events on feast days. My brothers and I were chosen to prepare children for first communion, and the older people helped prepare couples for marriage. When the army saw that the group kept growing and was taking part in more activities in the village, they didn't like it. We were accused of being a bad influence on the children.

In May 1981 a column of soldiers dressed as civilians arrived in our village. They singled out six of the leading catechists and kidnapped them; one of them was my uncle. Luckily we were not at home: at that time, many people were too frightened to spend the night in their houses, preferring to sleep under the coffee bushes some distance away. Those of the catechists who were in their homes were taken away by the army. We were hiding where we could see our house and the soldiers. First they went and got my uncle, then they came back down to our house. They didn't find my father, but they left the front door completely destroyed and our clothes strewn all over the place.

After they had gone, we found a blood-stained list that they had dropped. It contained the names of the catechists from each family, my family included. We decided to leave the village once and for all, but my father didn't want to go because we had fruit ready to harvest. So we left and he stayed behind ...

We went to Guatemala City where I met up with my husband who was involved in the same kind of work. Some time later he made a trip to our village to see his parents, while I visited another village nearby. I was nearly three months pregnant when I found out that he had been killed. They captured him in his parents' house. He tried to escape but he slipped and fell. They caught him and shot him once in the forehead, and he died on the spot. When I heard, I became terribly distressed and desperate. I felt that I couldn't live without him.

By the time I learned of my husband's death, the army had already started looking for me. When I heard this I decided to go to my mother in the capital. However, the only person who knew where she was living was my older brother, who was working in another part of Quiché, and I had to walk on my own for a whole day and a night to reach him. This involved crossing a huge river, which was really swollen because it was the rainy season. I don't know how to swim, so I just threw myself in with all my clothes on. At one point I felt that I was going under. The water carried me off and I said to myself, 'If I drown it will be better than the army getting hold of me.' But somehow I managed to cross the river and get to my brother's village. He advised me to stay and work there because it wasn't safe for me to go to the capital. The village was very isolated, with no transport, and there were sick people needing attention. I knew how to give injections and do some healing so I stayed.

I became very sad, losing all hope and feeling worthless. I couldn't bear the thought of what had happened to my husband. My brother was very supportive, and I stayed with him until I was in my seventh month, then I left for Guatemala City, where I felt a little better because I was with my mother. She was living there with my little brother in a house that some nuns had found for her. She couldn't speak Spanish, and I could speak only a very little. She hadn't been able to go out, even to the market, because the army was looking really hard for my family.

I had been in the city less than three months when the news arrived that my father had been kidnapped by the army. At first my mother was hopeful that he'd show up. Three days later we found out that he had been tortured and killed by the army. He had been captured in the village and taken to the convent [much church property was taken over by the military during the savage military campaign of the early 1980s and used for repressive purposes] along with 15 other people. They broke his arms and smashed his feet. They cut the flesh off his arm while he was still alive...

On 31 January 1982, my baby was born and a brother of mine was kidnapped. My brother was a student in the capital and he worked with the community. He left the house and never came back. He was 24 at the time. We named my baby after him.

Flight into Mexico
After all this, I couldn't stand it any more and I decided to leave the country. With the help of the nuns I got a passport and a 20-day tourist visa to Mexico. I left the country by bus on 20 February 1982, parting from my mother and sister-in-law without knowing whether we would ever see one another again.

We travelled along the coast. I had no experience of being a mother and I had this tiny baby with me. He started to cry and I didn't know what to do. An older man helped me out, telling me what to do for the baby. I had a woman accompanying me on the journey, but she sat in another part of the bus [for security reasons]. At one point the army boarded the bus and searched it. Everyone had to get off. Luckily, probably because of my baby who was asleep in my arms, as I was getting up to leave the bus the soldier told me to stay. Everyone else had to get off, and two men never got back on. They were taken away, and who knows what happened to them. They were probably killed ... Just into Mexico the immigration police boarded the bus and asked for our papers. 'Get your money out', they said. 'Anybody who can't pay stays here.' I had been lent some money for this purpose and I didn't even know how much Mexican money was worth, so I just gave them what they were asking for.

Our first home in Mexico was a very isolated village in the mountains. I found out that my grandparents had got there ahead of me, and then my mother and little brother came a month later. Our little house leaked when it rained. When the sun began to warm up the roof in the morning you could see snakes all over it. I was so scared that I couldn't sleep at night!

We had only been there six months when we were dealt another blow: we were told that my eldest brother had been killed, along with my sister-in-law, their eight-month-old baby and my aunt. They had been working with youth groups in the capital and teaching the Bible. Altogether, in my family they have killed my father, my husband, my two brothers, my uncle and aunt, and my nephew — an eight-month-old baby. That's how hard they have hit us. Despite all of this we carry on, and we still hope to go back to Guatemala one day.

We are the witnesses

We can't go back at the moment because when the army began to control the local population they organised civil patrols. People have to work for the army, some patrolling in the day and some at night. Those who don't comply with patrol duty are taken away and beaten or just 'disappeared'. The patrols have to watch out for guerrillas and make sure that they don't enter the village, because they are 'bad people, who kill you and carry out massacres'. This is not true, it's all lies. It's the army that does these things. It was they who burnt down our house and my grandparents' house, and destroyed the corn and beans that we had planted, and our clothes. We are the witnesses, and we can confirm that it is the army that does these things, not the guerrillas. In most villages it's not that easy to fool people into thinking that it's the guerrillas ... So the civil patrols are forced to patrol against their wishes.

In our village the army killed a lot of people. There are now a lot of widows, left with four or five children. My cousin, for example, was left a widow with eight children after they kidnapped and killed her husband. The saddest thing is that the soldiers and the military commissioners force the widows to become their women. It's the most awful thing, and it's done under threat. If a widow refuses to be the woman of the commissioner she'll be denounced. So people give in.

Surviving in exile

Here in Mexico we live off our weavings. I've learnt to speak Spanish, but we try not to forget our own language. My grandparents and I speak *Quiché* with each other and Spanish in public. Our basic foods in Guatemala were *tortillas*, chilli, salt and tomatoes, and we still eat them here. When we have time we buy the dough and make our *tortillas* by hand over an open fire. We don't use the stove much because we didn't have one in Guatemala and we are not very accustomed to it. We collect our own firewood in the hills nearby, and we still cultivate the land — we grow tomatoes and have a little corn plot.

Every month we have a meeting to discuss what is going on in our country. There's a group of five families, *Ixil* and *Quiché* Indians, living in this village and we meet and discuss among ourselves. We talk about our customs, the different customs of each village, things like that. We're learning about the different regions of Guatemala, and we are teaching the children. We also talk about all the awful things that have happened because it helps to ease the pain. Sometimes I feel very depressed, but afterwards I say to myself that there's nothing for it but to keep going and try and contribute what we can from here. Right now, for example, we are working on some weavings whose profits will go to support Guatemala's 'communities in resistance'. These communities are made up of internal refugees who didn't want to leave their country. They stayed behind but, since there was a lot of repression in their villages, they took refuge in the mountains. They are still there, mainly in the Quiché, because that's where there has been so much repression. The army doesn't know where the communities are because they are deep in the mountains and they take precautions. They come from many different ethnic groups: *Quiché, Mam, Cakchiquel, Kanjobal, Kekchí* and *Ixil.* No one is excluded because of their ethnic group. They all work the land, growing vegetables. Those who know how to read and write a bit are carrying out literacy training. Many children have been born there in the mountains. Most importantly, they are well-organised and active.*

My son says that he will go back to Guatemala one day. He's even asked me when I can send him on his own! He wants to know if his other grandparents are still alive. He wants to study and get ahead and then do the kind of work his father did — being a catechist and working the land. All the children here are very interested in their country. Yes, the children must return; there's no way that they can stay here.

*On September 7 1990 the Communities of People in Resistance (CPR) made a public declaration of their existence and demanded certain rights including: government recognition of their civilian status; an end to military attacks (including bombings) against them; and the right to return to their homes and lands free from military repression and interference.

Weavers of the future

In October 1987, nearly 1,500 women took part in the week-long Latin American and Caribbean feminist encounter held in Taxco, Mexico. Among those who attended was a group of Guatemalan Indian women living in exile in Mexico City, who had come together to form a weaving collective, called in *Quiché* the *Ja C'Amabal I'B* workshop. Their idea was to support themselves with their traditional craft of weaving, while at the same time carrying out political work involving both Indians and women. All the women involved in the workshop have had to flee their native Guatemala. Elena, a 23-year-old *Ixil* Indian from Quiché province, is a founding member of the collective.

In 1976 the army took over my village, and as a result the whole community became organised. I joined the Committee for Peasant Unity (CUC). By 1982 the repression was so harsh that a group of us decided to occupy the Brazilian embassy to let the world know what was going on in Guatemala.

There were 13 of us: nine men and four women. The women were about my age — I was 16 at the time. We wanted to hold a press conference to denounce the repression, and then to leave for another country afterwards. If we had remained in Guatemala after occupying the embassy we definitely wouldn't have survived. The government, however, refused to negotiate with us in any way whatsoever and the army surrounded the embassy with tanks. We were in the embassy for two days and one night. The ambassador was ill and the embassy staff were afraid after what had happened at the Spanish embassy in 1980. [In a peaceful occupation of the Spanish embassy in 1980, some 39 people presenting similar demands were burned to death in a police attack on the embassy building.]

We were not permitted to hold the press conference, but after the Brazilian ambassador intervened we were allowed to leave the country. The Mexican government offered us political asylum. We left the embassy on the night of the second day, but found ourselves on our own at the airport. The government said that our aeroplane had faults and couldn't leave, so we had to spend the night there. This was a way of punishing us and also an attempt to pressure us into staying in Guatemala. It was in the government's interest for us to stay, because then it would appear that we had been lying about repression. General Ríos Montt came to the plane twice to talk to us and ask us why we wouldn't stay. He said that they would give us amnesty and work, and that we would be set free. Nobody wanted to stay. So, finally, in the early hours of the morning, the plane took off.

Exiled in Mexico City

We landed in Mexico City. It was awful. Although I had joined the CUC when I was 14 years old, the truth is I had never been out of my village, apart from one visit to the provincial capital with my father. Coming to Mexico City was a very radical change.

At first the Mexican government put us up in a hotel. We were shut up in it for over two months and told that it would be dangerous for us to go out since the Guatemalan government might make an attempt on our lives. Sometimes we were taken out for a walk but we were always brought straight back. After about three months we were allowed to leave the hotel and we went to live with some friends who had a house and a job.

Little by little we got to know the city. I didn't speak Spanish very well. It was very difficult, riding the metro and buying things. I wasn't familiar with the money. In the street I felt as if I was dumb — I wouldn't speak because I was afraid I might be identified as Guatemalan. I didn't even dare ask people the time or directions. The thing that most frightened me was the traffic. Even if I was at the traffic lights and had the right to cross I always ran across the road.

I hardly knew the people that I had left with and the people that I met here at first were all from Guatemala City or the coast. The thing is that if you are Indian you always feel inferior. It's drummed into you from an early age that because you are an Indian, you are inferior, illiterate and ignorant. Even if you don't really believe it, you can't help internalising it. So I always felt inferior to the other *compañeros* and lonely because I had left my people behind. I haven't seen any of my family in the seven years I've been here. Yes, it was very difficult at the beginning, and it still is.

I feel that I have changed considerably. You learn a lot from being here: you are not so timid, you become a bit more daring. Speaking in public is very difficult for me but now I am doing it, whereas before I never would have. I've learnt about a lot of things — in fact, I've learnt more about Guatemala here than I did there.

Weaving in the city

In 1985 I became involved in the weaving workshop. Some other women and I decided that we couldn't carry on working in houses, taking care of other people's children and cleaning. We realised that we had our own artisan work: we could weave. So we started to make small wall-hangings and people took them to the United States and sold them for us. The problem was that the money arrived late or got lost on the way. So we decided that we would find a market here in Mexico, and that we ourselves would organise any sales abroad. There are five women and one man involved in the day-to-day production of our weaving workshop. We are interested in the Indian question, and the original idea behind forming the workshop was to be able to work on this issue in addition to producing our weavings.

I love weaving. I began to weave when I was seven. I can weave anything and embroider as well. But in Guatemala there would be five of us weaving together. My mother and my grandmother would be around and so would other people. It was more sociable. We often wove on the patio under the trees and it was good fun. In Mexico City it is different — we started off in an apartment. We had the warp tied to the window-pane and we were always afraid of making too much noise and disturbing our neighbours. We felt uncomfortable — it wasn't how we had done it in Guatemala.

Everything that we Indians weave is related to nature: eagles, horses, volcanoes, birds ... things like that. We don't weave anything else. I always weave *Ixil* designs and colours. I have learnt weaving designs from Chichicastenango from a friend here, but I don't do them. I believe that since I am an *Ixil*, I'm not going to weave something that's not *Ixil*. I don't even have to think about it twice.

I don't wear my *traje* here. It's not possible. It's very hard for me because it is instilled in us that we are Indian, and that our identity comes from our *traje*, from our language, and from our community.

69

By 1980 if you wore an *Ixil traje* you were automatically regarded as a guerrilla. I wear these clothes, trousers, because I have to. But I don't feel right. I have stored my *traje* away, but sometimes, when I can, I put it on for a while. When I picture myself in Guatemala, I always see myself in my *traje*. I believe that I will go back to the village where I was born and see my family one day, but only when the military is no longer there. If that's not possible, then I might go to another region and wear the *traje* from there.

To most people in Guatemala, the Indian is ignorant and illiterate. So, when they see an Indian like me who can speak Spanish, who wears glasses and a watch, they say I am no longer an Indian. But it doesn't make any difference — I can wear these things and know how to operate a computer, and I will still be Indian. The fact that Indians improve themselves and get ahead doesn't mean that they are not Indians. It depends on what you feel and your identity with your people, your culture and your ancestors.

Indians are involved in the struggle, but what is it that they really want? We began to analyse this in the weaving workshop, to put forward different ideas and to talk to Indians from other groups. Then we thought, 'We're talking about Indians in general, but what about Indian women?' Indian women carry two or three times the load because we have to struggle against racial and sexual discrimination. But we believe that Indian women have a right to organise as women ... In the workshop, we soon realised that we women were the ones doing most of the work — not only producing the weavings, but doing the political and solidarity work as well. We became aware of our abilities. We weren't women 'fit for nothing but housework, who can't think, who are backward' — all the awful things they say about women. But when we began talking about women's situation, many Indian *compañeros* said, 'What kind of women are these?', and started running us down.

If I went back...
If I were to go back to my village the first problem would be to see how my own community would accept me as a woman who had left. I remember when my sisters went away to study, people said, 'Who knows what they'll get up to there, or what bad habits they might pick up.' So I would have to see how they would react to me...

I would have to win their trust, to behave and talk in a certain way. If I were working with women, for example, I couldn't start to talk to them about sex because they would tell me to get lost. I remember when some women from the capital came to my village once and talked to us about menstruation. Our mothers all became angry and said they were teaching us bad things. They aren't bad things, but...

Intimate relations between Indians appear to be very cold. The men themselves don't know what sex is. A psychologist in the mental health group told us that many men, *ladino* as well as Indian *campesinos*, only feel that they have something down there that they have to relieve. They are not aware that they could do other things, that there are other sensations.

For example, in my village people don't kiss. You never see Indians holding hands or kissing each other in public. They sometimes even say not to let a man touch your hand, because if you do you'll get pregnant! It's not because people don't feel the desire to kiss or embrace each other, it's the indoctrination that they get. The church did a good job at changing them so that they only believe in God and think everything else is a sin.

Many women say that when they got married, they never felt anything during sex with their husbands. They say that they used to wait for the men to go to sleep before they went to bed, so that nothing would happen. They dread it rather than look forward to it. It's fear, really.

This is all beginning to change. I can talk to men about these things nowadays, and the majority of Guatemalan women here in exile, both Indian and *ladina*, use contraception now. With respect to abortion, however, certain Indian *compañeras* believe that they will be punished, that they are killing the child inside them. For example, I met an Indian *compañera* recently in one of the women's groups. She already had a small child and didn't want another one because she wanted to better herself and participate more. Her husband was no help to her in any way. She asked us what she should do, and we said that if she wanted to have an abortion she should go ahead and have one. So she did. But I think she felt guilty afterwards.

This attitude has a lot to do with the Catholic religion. It is not part of our indigenous culture, because I remember women in my village having as many as twelve children and asking, 'What can I do?' As no contraception was available, they couldn't do anything. Also, there was the church saying that this is a sin, and that you should have all the children God sends you. It's a problem. It is changing now, but it's a very gradual process...

A different feminism

In 1987, the workshop was invited to take part in the Fourth Feminist encounter held in Taxco, the four of us from the collective went. We gave a presentation in which we analysed our experience, our development and how we had become conscious as Indian women. We also put forward our demands. We were the only Indian women's group at the conference. Four women came from inside Guatemala, but they were *ladinas* from the popular organisations. We began to find out about the problems of women in other countries, their kinds of organisations and their demands. This made us ask ourselves what we had achieved as indigenous women.

Through the discussions that took place, we realised that women themselves, Indian women included, reproduce their own oppression — in the way they bring up their children, for example. There are many things, which if they are not questioned will reproduce the same oppression.

The Indian woman suffers from a triple exploitation by virtue of being a woman, being Indian and being poor. We have to find a way of combating these three problems simultaneously. That's why our workshop's declaration contains a class position, an ethnic position and a gender position. If we were to carry on a separate fight for women's liberation, we wouldn't resolve anything, we'd be wasting our time.

Our workshop started to meet with other groups of Guatemalan women in Mexico. We formed an organisation called *Nan*, meaning 'mother' in *Quiché*, to work with the children of Guatemalans living in Mexico who were learning a different culture in Mexican schools. Then we began to question what was happening to the children's mothers. We contacted other women's groups, and when larger meetings were held we found that we always ended up talking about the same thing: the problem of roles.

Today *Nan* is made up of the representatives of various Guatemalan women's organisations, each of which has its own demands and objectives. We want women to become conscious of themselves as women, to discover and fight for their objectives.

There isn't a lot of difference between the Guatemalan women's groups here in Mexico and the ones in Guatemala. We are striving for the same things. Here we have more possibilities because we can organise bigger activities where 40 or 50 women might be present. This would not be possible inside Guatemala because of the security problems. Groups without office space hold meetings in their houses, but when a lot of people are seen entering and leaving a house the army starts watching it. Also, the National Women's Office (Onam), which is run by the Christian Democrat party, accused one women's group of being a 'clandestine organisation' because they don't act in the same way as they do, nor do they have a proper office ... The women connected with the Onam are not women who have suffered from poverty and discrimination.

Our women's groups seem to be quite different from those in the United States. They focus on other issues. The situation in Central America is very different from that in other countries, and I believe that we will have to create a different kind of feminism. We have so many problems, and what we are seeing with Guatemalan women nowadays is not that they are leaving the class struggle, but that they are fighting for their own demands at the same time. They know that if they don't they are not going to achieve anything.

Sexual discrimination exists everywhere, including within the class struggle. There are *compañeros* who are very aware, but at the level of class consciousness, nothing else. They still don't regard women as their equals. They have not stopped thinking of us as sexual objects, and this is the level on which they always relate to us at first, without thinking about our ability or what we can contribute.

Many women get aggressive when they see this. I believe that we have to confront this ideologically, not by attacking men, but by discussing it with them so that they will understand. Their response is natural — it's been around for centuries. All of us have to become more aware.

It is similar with the Indian question. Many people involved in the national liberation struggle claim that they understand, and that they don't discriminate against us. If you listen to them, however, and the way they talk about Indians, their racism sometimes slips out without their wanting it to. We are the ones who suffer this ... Take the example of the *ladina* who was invited to go on a speaking tour of Europe in 1980. She was very conscious of our situation but presented an Indian woman to the audience by saying: 'This is a

Guatemalan Indian, this is what they look like, they wear *traje*, they speak various languages and now she's going to give you her testimony.' The Indian woman didn't know how to deal with this. She packed her bags and returned to Guatemala, furious because she was presented like this and limited to giving testimony. Another Indian woman had a similar experience when a group of Guatemalans were invited to go to New York, and the Indian woman was told that she couldn't accompany them because 'this time it wasn't about giving testimony'.

Presenting women as 'victims' goes hand-in-hand with discrimination. Unfortunately, this still goes on practically everywhere. The woman gives testimony and the man gives analysis. From our point of view, this cannot continue. We can continue to give testimony, but we can also provide analysis and even write books. We must become the protagonists in our own struggle.

3
FAMILY AFFAIRS

Marrying for love

A 25-year-old *Achi* indian, who works as a coffee picker, talks about marriage.

There are some of our customs that I don't agree with, such as not marrying for love. I didn't even know the man who wanted to marry me. All of a sudden, my parents asked me if I wanted to get married. The assumption was that I would. I was very obstinate because I had seen how it was when my sister got married. She hadn't wanted to, but my parents took the decision and told her afterwards. She cried and cried. One day they fixed up the altar in the house very prettily and people brought her lots of present, then the next day there she was in the church, getting married with her eyes swollen from weeping. Half-way through the mass, the priest asked her, 'Are you getting married of your own free will?' and she replied, 'Yes, father.' I was so furious, because I knew how she had cried. If it had been me, I wouldn't have cared, I'd have said 'No', right there at the altar.

No, I've been stubborn. When my parents asked me if I liked the man, I said that I didn't. So, here I am, and I'm only going to marry someone that I want to.

Catholics and sexuality

A 49-year-old *ladina* lawyer talks about *ladina* families and sexuality.

The family is too strong in Guatemala. I'm always complaining that I can't find any men here. I can find males, yes, but not men. I mean someone who stands up for you, who gives you priority over everyone else, who makes you feel that you are the person closest to him. This is very difficult to find in Guatemala, where families are so close that most men are 'mummy's boys'. They tend to want to find a replica of their own mother in their wives.

I think that this is related to most of us being Catholics. Catholics have an objection to good sex. They feel that sex is something that should be done in order to have children. This has caused many men and women to have incestuous feelings. They don't act on them, of course, because of the morality imposed by the Catholic religion.

We are living a big farce. You see lots of marriages where the people are just together because that's the way it's supposed to be, not because the husband and wife have a good relationship. Children are dominated by their parents until they die. People never seem to really grow up, to truly become independent, and this has caused many of us who do become independent to have problems.

'The only thing women need men for is martyrdom'

In makeshift shacks tucked into ravines and under bridges, many of Guatemala's urban poor eke out their existence in the ever-growing number of shantytowns that surround the capital. These squatter settlements mushroom on vacant lots which, for a variety of reasons, are not used by their owners. In many instances, the construction of more permanent housing and services is blocked by these landowners, anxious to evict the squatters and recuperate their assets.

The hastily erected 'temporary' shelters may often house two or three generations of a family before a land dispute is resolved. In the meantime, the shantytown continues to grow, taking on a semblance of permanency. In the more organised settlements, neighbourhood committees are formed, sometimes aided by social workers and religious groups. These seek to develop a sense of community and to improve living conditions by trying to get the most basic services installed.

In one such shantytown, built on the side of a steep ravine less than a mile from Guatemala City's National Palace, the effects of such organisation can be seen in the neat, well-constructed Nutrition Centre that dominates the entrance to the settlement. Surrounded by unpaved streets and ramshackle, teetering housing, the centre provides balanced meals for most of the young children that live in this neighbourhood. It is also a meeting place where residents can learn new skills and hold discussions on topics relevant to their situation.

Claudia, a 54-year-old *ladina* kitchen assistant at the centre, has lived in this shantytown for nearly 30 years. She chooses the larder of the centre as the quietest place for an interview. There, amongst the huge baskets of carrots and onions, with continuous interruptions from children who obviously adore her, she talks about her disastrous marriage. Her story is not uncommon of the women who live in these slums, where alcoholism and violence are rampant.

The most important thing in my life for the last eight years has been looking after the children at the centre and serving the community. I never participated in anything before. Nobody liked me. Then Ana, who works at the centre with us, talked to me for ages about coming to the centre. So I thought, why not?

I've changed as a result. I've learnt a lot from the talks on nutrition, on how to treat children and on relationships. Before, when I stayed at home, I was on my own with just the four walls of my room. I saw nothing. People could collapse in front of me and it was all the same to me. I would have passed them by. Not now — now, what happens to a fellow being happens to me.

I'm not religious. I go to Mass from time to time, but that's not being religious. Catholics keep all the commandments and go to Mass on holy days, for baptisms and on Sundays. To me that's not a good thing. They might go to Mass, but perhaps they don't help their fellows. What's the good of being in Mass if somebody needs your help? Somebody might need refreshment, food, and if I'm in Mass I won't see that. Evangelicals pray and pray, and make a lot of noise, but they don't see the reality around them, the work to be done with one's neighbour. For me the best religion is helping others, the community.

The family

I don't think I've had a good life. There are always problems with one's husband and children. My relationship with my husband has been difficult because he drinks. When a man drinks too much he loses his sense of morality. My husband tries to beat me, but I don't let him. When he comes home drunk, he is very sexually demanding. That's why we have had problems. Ana says that he must have traumatised me the first time. She says that there are people who feel desire for their husbands. But I never have, never, ever.

At the beginning I loved him a lot. But after the first time, when I knew what it meant to have a husband, I didn't want him. When he wanted to be with me there were always arguments. I was only 17 when we got married, but he was 28. The thing is, in a village one is brought up in ignorance. My mother never allowed me to go out anywhere, to parties or anything, so I wasn't very smart and I took the first man that came along. I did love him then, though.

We had been going together since I was 13. He was my first boyfriend.

Over the years I have thought of leaving him. But my grandmother talked me out of it. She said, 'Look, if he doesn't treat you too badly, or call you bad names, then don't leave him. You are just a kid and you'll only end up with somebody else who'll do what he pleases with you...'

My children are grown up and married now, but my husband treats them as if they were the lowest of the low. I don't let them fight or argue with him, though, because I don't want them to hurt or accidentally kill him, as then they would have to go to prison.

The truth is I still want to leave, to disappear, for him not to be able to find me. But I'm older now, and it would be awful to end up as an old woman on my own. He has become worse as he has got older, but you can't just go around changing from one man to another. Nobody needs a man, but there is always one of them running after you. The only thing women need men for is martyrdom...

Maybe there are marriages that are happy, because I see that some couples get on well. They understand each other, they do things together, the husband respects the woman. I don't know if this is luck or what, but I haven't experienced it.

Alcohol changed my husband. He wasn't so aggressive before as he is now. When I come home late, he's sitting there drunk and he starts asking me where I've been and who I've been with. He goads me and he tries to hit me... He knows full well where I've been, what time I leave work and why I arrive late. I tell him that he has no right to say anything to me, that if he doesn't want me to go out to work he should give me my housekeeping money. If I had everything I needed here, then I wouldn't go out. That's when he gets angry and treats me badly. It's not that he doesn't trust me. If he really mistrusted me he would have killed me by now. Anyway, I've never met a man that I got on well with — maybe because of the bad luck I've had with my husband. Other men have approached me, but I've never let my husband down in this way. Still, I agree that he should beat me if I show him a lack of respect. There are married women who go with other men and I think that if their husbands find out they should beat them.

Some women here are confused about women's liberation. They think that liberation means the freedom to do whatever they please.

I think a woman has to be responsible towards both her husband and her children. She has to look after the household. I know I go out to work, but I always take care of the house. I wash the clothes and I keep my house tidy. I spend every Sunday cleaning the house. Women don't have the same freedom as men. The same rights, maybe, but we are looked down upon. Our dignity is taken away from us.

Family planning

A 42-year-old *ladina* woman living in exile in the United States discusses family planning in Guatemala.

The basic thing in family planning is education. When you know what is available to you and what is behind family planning then you can decide how many children you want. But it must be your decision, not Aprofam's (the Pro-Family Welfare Association). These contraception programmes really put a lot of pressure on women, and they misinform them. They try to make families feel guilty by saying that the reason why the country is not making progress is because we have a lot of children, and that's just not true. I think that we should have as many children as we can handle, but let's not be saying that a family is irresponsible because they have a lot of children and they are poor. We should have choice based on proper education — not because we see a commercial on TV, and not because a family-planning organisation says that two is the ideal number of children. I hate the kind of subtle propaganda that comes through the movies and TV: the ideal family — a woman, a man and two children.

Abortion has existed for a very long time in Guatemala and women have them with or without the approval of the church. Information and legislation is important if a woman is to go to the right place and not harm herself. I have heard of many women who arrive at the General Hospital bleeding to death. Many have died because they did their abortions themselves, or else somebody without experience did it.

Abortion will provoke a lot of debate in Guatemala: it is such a difficult issue.

Children bless a home

A 46-year-old *ladina* market woman and mother of five talks about contraception.

I'm not sure about contraception. Sometimes I think the way the economic situation is these days you should avoid having more children. Especially women who already have four, five, or six. But for those who have only one, I don't think it's a good idea.

These pills and all these treatments they give here damage your health. Something goes wrong with you, and you find out it's due to these. Also, I've been told that taking these pills causes children to be born deformed ... But it's better to take precautions than to commit a sin when you have already conceived. I don't believe that we should conceive and not give birth. Children bless a home, we achieve a lot through them. A home without children is like a silent forest. A child brings happiness to a home and keeps the parents together. I know many single mothers, and it makes me proud to see them with their children, working hard and bringing them up, but some of them don't want their children. They give them away or abandon them.

Contraception causes a lot of wantonness. There are women who want to make love and not have children. That is not correct for a woman. For me, we should have children and raise them. That is why God made us women and why we have husbands. But sometimes the woman suffers because of her husband's lack of responsibility — if he's a drunk, for example, and doesn't provide food. Then it's better to avoid having children. It's worse to see a child suffer than to not have one. You have to think about contraception carefully because children are not toys or puppies, they are human. If I had a husband who wasn't responsible, I wouldn't have children.

But a woman is a woman and she has to have her children — and when the father is a responsible person I think that we should have all the children that God gives us, because that's what marriage is about. Then we can live happily, even though we may be poor and eat only beans or chilli and tomatoes...

FIGHTING BACK

Until we find them

In June 1984, some two dozen people, the overwhelming majority of whom were Guatemala City housewives, formed what has become the most vocal human rights organisation in Guatemala's history: the Mutual Support Group (Gam). Its members are relatives of Guatemala's estimated 42,000 'disappeared'.

While the founders of the Gam were primarily *ladina* city dwellers, the ranks soon grew to include many Indian women — without doubt the sector most affected by the policy of forced disappearances. The brutal murders of two Gam leaders in March 1985, intended to put an end to the organisation, had the opposite effect as more and more relatives of disappeared people joined the Gam, increasing membership to over 1,000 by 1986. More recent killings and disappearances of Gam members, as well as the constant death threats received by the leadership, have not succeeded in silencing the Gam's demands for an official explanation of what has happened to their relatives.

The Gam's endurance is due in part to the international support that it has received. Recognition of its members' courage and determination has come in the form of international awards. In addition 56 British parliamentarians proposed the Gam as a candidate for the Nobel Peace Prize in 1986.

Ester, who is a founder member of the Gam, is a working-class *ladina* housewife in her 60s.

I've been a member of the Mutual Support Group (Gam) since the day it was founded. I have just been looking through some of my son's papers, his study records, personal things... I like to do this when I have some free time, to remind me of him. Not that I don't remember him, but this helps me to keep his image alive in my mind. I only do it when I feel really strong and know that it won't make me cry.

My son, Jorge Alberto Herrate, was abducted on 15 May 1983. It was during the regime of General Efraín Ríos Montt, of which we have terrible memories. He was dragged out of this house in front of my husband and me. It was about 6.40pm but it was still light outside. It had been a very hot day so we had the front door open. I was still in the kitchen and we had just finished supper. My son was watching television when the men came into the house without saying a word. There were two of them. My son is not very tall, about 5ft 5in. These men were tall and armed. As they were the ones with the guns and our door was open it was pointless to try and hide. One trained his enormous gun on us from the doorway. Although they were wearing civilian clothes, which is common in these cases, they belonged to the government security forces. The only words spoken were when the man who was pointing his gun at us told us to close the door. I ran after him into the garden to see what was happening. I tried to grab hold of my son, but I was threatened by the other man with his gun. They took him away in a small mustard-coloured car. I saw three other cars behind the house, one of which was a large, elegant dark-coloured one, and I also saw more armed men... The neighbours and passers-by witnessed everything because it was still daylight. But it is difficult to ask people to testify because it is very risky.

My son was working for the Western Oil petroleum company at the time. He had just come home the day before. He worked out on the site (at Rubelsalto in the Peten) for three weeks at a time, then he would get a week off... He was 29 years old and married. His wife and two little girls weren't here that night. They were in Chicago visiting his wife's family and were due back the following day. They came as planned and stayed until November. But Magda, my daughter-in-law, couldn't find a job that paid enough here, so what with that and the personal insecurity she went to the United States. In Guatemala she ran the risk of being abducted as well and of something awful happening to her children.

As soon as they had taken my son, my husband went straight to the police to report it. He went to all the different police forces and, as they usually do in these cases, they all said they would investigate. The next day we went to see a lawyer to draw up a declaration to take to the Tribunal Tower. The judge who attended to us made us pay 50 *quetzales*, which is completely illegal, but you think that by paying the money you will get some sort of response...

On 19 May my children who live in the United States went to Americas Watch, to the Washington Office on Latin America, and to US congressmen to denounce what had happened. I went to the Venezuelan and Canadian embassies here. I knew that the petroleum companies belong to these countries, so I went to beg them to do something, to intercede with the Guatemalan government so that my son might reappear. I also had meetings with Lord Colville [then UN Special Rapporteur on Guatemala] when he visited here to ask him to intervene and help find my son. It was all totally useless...

I went to the morgues; I saw hundreds of corpses... I spent ten months going around the morgues. I had mixed feelings about it: I wanted to find something, even if it was only his body, but at the same time I prayed that he was still alive. When I saw the atrocities and the mutilated bodies, it sent shivers down my spine. I felt so depressed that I thought I would lose my mind...

A few days after Jorge had been abducted a man came to my house. He was very courteous and he brought proof that he was a colleague of my son's, so I trusted him. He spun me a long tale about how he had influential friends and could discover Jorge's whereabouts and probably even obtain his release.

He came to my house every day for six months. I think now that he must have been sent to keep an eye on me. How else could anyone have left their job for so long? He even came on Sundays and holidays. His name was Jorge Federico Yaxcal Arriaga and he was from Cobán. He wore the same kind of boots as the military wear and sometimes he was armed. But he told me he was a military commissioner, so I didn't think anything of it. He asked me for money on several occasions, supposedly to travel to Esquintla and other areas of the country to see if he could find Jorge. Then he told me that Jorge was being held in the General Military Barracks — that they had him working there and that he was fine. Believing that at least my son was alive, I gave this man clothes and other personal things to pass on to him. Then one day the man phoned me and told me to come to the Pavón prison to see him. He'd been arrested for not keeping up his child support payments. When I went to see him he swore that what he had said was true. He even cried. But when he got out of prison, I never saw him again. He was an imposter and he swindled us.

Formation of the Gam

In May 1984, when I was desperate at my inability to find my son, and all my knocking on doors and appealing to people's humanity was having no effect, I was invited to a special Mass for the disappeared. There I met Nineth Montenegro de Garcia and many others with the same problem. Some people's faces were already known to me from visits to morgues and different detention centres... We were the people who would later form the Gam. After the Mass some of us got together, mainly women: the sisters, wives and mothers of the disappeared. Nineth called on us to unite and ask the government to investigate our cases and tell us where our loved ones were. So the Gam was founded about a year after my son was abducted. I was one of the first members.

Of course we were afraid, but our love for our relatives made us feel that together we would be able to protect each other. It was an encounter of people who had gone through the same things, who had suffered the same pain. We understood each other and we were considerate to each other. That's how our name arose: the *Mutual Support Group*. It expresses what we are.

The Gam started, naturally, at the most elementary level. We asked for audiences with the Minister of the Interior and the then Head of State, General Oscar Mejía Víctores, who received us twice and listened to our painful stories. He said that he would investigate them, but nothing happened. The Minister did not even try to appear benevolent. He said that our loved ones had gone to the United States clandestinely to find work. But I had proof that this was not so. My son had studied geology in the United States, so he had a valid passport with a current US visa. He had no need to enter the US illegally. In any case, I was there when he was taken away and I don't have the slightest doubt that the people who took him belonged to the government forces.

The Gam continues to make its demands to the authorities, but they have all been in vain. We meet regularly, every Saturday. We plan demonstrations every Friday in the central plaza. Our first march was in October 1984 and we marched 29 kilometres (18 miles) from San Lucas to Guatemala City. A lot of people accompanied us, religious people, workers and *campesinos*.

I was a member of the executive committee of the Gam until my husband died last year. I took part in our occupation of the National Palace. The police treated us really badly and beat us up. We were also beaten during other demonstrations that we held at the entrance to the Palace. My house was under surveillance for three years. I don't know if it still is, because with the sports facilities nearby people can pass by unnoticed. Previously, it was very obvious because it was always the same person in front of the house.

Living with loss

Living with the uncertainty of a loved one's whereabouts causes terrible anguish. You have no appetite, you can't sleep at night because you are always on edge, thinking that your loved one could come home at any moment. You're attentive to the slightest noise in the street. A car drawing up, a knock on a door... Day by day the suffering undermines your health. I believe that this is what caused my husband's illness — he couldn't stand the grief. What they say about forgetting with time is false. We will never, ever forget. In my case, as a mother — a woman — I conceived my son, I anxiously awaited his birth and after he was born I brought him up with love.

My son was very studious; he got his education through scholarships. He had a state scholarship for six years because he was such a bright student... The company he worked for sent him to do further studies in petroleum and geology. The most recent courses he did were in Houston. He always excelled as a student.

I've spent many long days and sleepless nights thinking over all the possible reasons why they took him away, and this is the conclusion I've come to. He worked in the countryside, which is where there is the most poverty and hunger in Guatemala. I think that he must have witnessed something — the scorched-earth tactics or one of the massacres that the different military governments, and the civilian government, have committed. If you see a massacre — well, they don't want any witnesses. My son wasn't connected with any political group. He worked for weeks on end; when he came back to the city we would go out and do things together, and he looked after his wife and family. Maybe he saw something, or maybe he tried to defend someone...

We don't really expect to find our relatives alive now. At this stage, who could have survived for so long? But I cherish the hope that at least I'll find my son's remains. Although it is extremely painful, we have asked the government to tell us whether our relatives are alive or dead, and if they are dead, to tell us why. But this is a problem: after all, what reply can the government give us?

It is not going to admit in front of the international community that it killed them.

Some journalists once asked General Mejía Víctores what response he had for the Gam, and he replied that the army had done what it had done because if it hadn't we would now be living under a communist regime. He was giving us to understand that they had killed the disappeared because they considered them subversive, communists... Here in Guatemala, anybody who asks for a salary rise or says that hunger or illiteracy exists is accused of being a communist.

I will go on demanding an answer from the government. I'm not going to give up. As long as I live, I will do the same. We want to know what happened to our relatives, and if justice exists we will demand justice. I am not talking about revenge. They tell us that the Gam demonstrations are illegal but I ask myself, 'When they took our relatives away, was that legal?' The Gam has been slandered: they say we are trying to destabilise the government. We are not demanding a change in government. What we are demanding is a clarification. When they took away a loved one, they took away half of our lives — that's how we feel. What some think is courage is not so. It's love, love for the person who was taken away.

My life has changed immensely. My house is depressing, there is no gaiety because the whole family has been affected. We live, because we have to live. But we have suffered so deeply that our lives have completely changed... Before, I was a very happy person, I liked to go out, to go on trips. The last holiday I had was in April 1983, when we went with Jorge and his family to the seaside. Since then, I haven't been away. At first, it was because I thought he might come back at any minute and I wanted to wait for him. These days I suffer from nervous-type ailments and the only time I go out is to Gam activities and to church.

I feel good going on our demonstrations. On 10 December, the day commemorating the Declaration of Human Rights, we marched from Zone 13 to the National Palace. We know full well that what we are doing is a hopeless sacrifice. The government couldn't care less about what it costs us, both physically and mentally. Yet I feel that this activity is positive, that at least I am doing something. For me, it's a moral obligation that I owe to my son and his daughters. The Gam slogan is 'until we find them', so we are not going to give up.

Fighting in the Guerrilla Army of the Poor

During the late-1970s, the western highlands of Guatemala were plunged into what one army colonel described as a state of 'near total war'. The first actions carried out by the Guerrilla Army of the Poor (EGP) in 1975 met with a swift response from the Guatemalan military, who swarmed into the area to carry out aerial bombings and occupy numerous mountain villages. From then on, the local population (about 90 per cent Indian) became the focus of Central America's most sophisticated counter-insurgency war, a war which the military waged unhindered by the most basic tenets of human rights.

In 1977 the Guatemalan army rejected all US military aid in order to avoid imminent congressional restrictions linking future bilateral aid to respect for human rights. The result was a bloodbath, with tens of thousands of Indians massacred. The army itself points to some 440 villages that were completely destroyed. An estimated 45,000 women were widowed and as many as 200,000 children lost one or both parents in the violence.

Hundreds of *campesinos* flocked to join guerrilla organisations in an attempt to defend themselves against the army's onslaught. These organisations, they hoped, would be instrumental in forging a new, more just society in which poor people would no longer be marginalised. Many of those who joined were very young Indian women who had previously led extremely sheltered lives in their villages. Dolores is an *Ixil* Indian who joined the EGP in 1980.

When I was 14 years old I stopped wearing my *traje* because I joined the guerrilla. I had to wear trousers. I wrapped my *traje* in a sheet along with my long earrings. 'Who knows if I'll ever wear these again', I thought to myself. 'I could die and never come back.' I sent the bundle to my house with some *compañeros* and put on trousers. I felt awful, but good at the same time because I was finally going to fight. I had seen all the injustice in my village.

In 1976, one of my uncles and two of my cousins who belonged to popular organisations were abducted by the army. 'We can't do anything here anymore', I said to my father. 'They are kidnapping everyone who stays behind. I want to leave and get trained so that I'll be able to do something.'

My father belonged to one of the popular organisations. In the beginning he had had a lot of faith in political parties. He stood as candidate to be mayor of our village and won, but right-wing parties defrauded him of his votes. Then he said that nothing could be done through political parties, because the people who were appointed to local posts never did anything. He wanted the community to progress, for drinking water to be installed and a road to be built. But he didn't want me to join the guerrilla. 'What can you do?' he said. 'You are only a woman!' There were five of us sisters, but only two of us enlisted. The others weren't interested. My father wouldn't give my sister and me permission to leave, but we used to buy sugar and other things for the *companeros* and take it into the hills for them. They were about a day's walk away. My father said that this could be bad for us because women are not used to walking long distances or withstanding the cold. But we put on our boots, along with our *cortes*, and off we went. Eventually my father stopped objecting, but he still wouldn't let me join up. In the end I went without saying anything to my family. I joined with my cousin, not my sister.

When I arrived at the guerrilla camp I was really happy. I had wanted to fight alongside them for a long time, especially as I'd been told that women weren't up to it and I was determined that I would be. Since I was very young I had wanted to fight and to do something different from what the other girls did. At age 14, they were asking me why I wasn't getting married!

At the first camp I was in there were many women, *ladinas* and Indians from different ethnic groups. It was good that there were so many women. We began to talk among each other even though at the time I didn't speak much Spanish and didn't say much. Most of us were very young, the oldest being only about 25 ... Yet I have always felt grown up and behaved in a responsible way. I never played or did things that young people do.

After I had been in the camp for a while, I saw that the men were the ones going off to do guard duty. I wanted to do it, too. But they didn't want me to go. They said that I was new and had to learn how to handle a weapon and be trained. The training was difficult, but I did everything. It was hard. We had to get up at 6 o'clock and do exercises. The women did exactly the same exercises as the men; the groups were mixed... At the beginning I was frightened that the army would come, but later I lost my fear. One of the best days for me was the day I was given my own gun. There were many women but only three of us were chosen to receive guns: myself, my cousin and another woman. We were given UZIs, small machine guns. I was very happy because I knew that if we were attacked I would be able to do something.

A big advantage that we women had was the support of local people. Often when we arrived in a village, its people (who generally couldn't afford to eat meat) would kill one of their animals for us. They were very fond of us, particularly the women. 'You are so young', they would say. 'What are you doing here?' This would inspire us. They weren't afraid of us — on the contrary, when other women and young people saw us they wanted to join too.

All the walking we had to do was hard, and I became a bit disillusioned because the *compañeros*, who were mostly *campesinos*, were able to walk such long distances even at night. Sometimes we women got left behind and the men would say, 'Hang on, the tortoises are falling behind'. I would get very angry and say that since they knew how, they ought to teach us. Since women are usually confined to the house we are not as used to walking long distances. But, after a while we learned how and we became as good as them.

All tasks were distributed equally between squads of men and women; one squad would go for firewood and another would grind corn or fetch water. Men cooked as well. All the work was shared and that was really nice, but we never dealt with it as an issue — we never stated that this is how things should be, and that we would all have to change in order to form a new equal society of men and women. As a result, when the man was no longer in that particular camp he behaved like a *macho* and stopped doing those tasks because he had never been doing them out of awareness, but rather to fulfil orders. When I was moved to another front the men in that camp didn't do the cooking and would tell me or the other women to cook them breakfast.

I was in the guerrilla for two years before I became ill and had to leave the mountains ... Afterwards it was very difficult for me to adjust to the fact that I had more in common with men than with women. In some camps I had been the only woman in a platoon. Living side by side with men, going through danger together and being hungry together unites you and makes you identify with each other. Everything that happened to me there will affect me for the rest of my life.

Sisterhood is great

Although most of those who fled the political violence in Guatemala have found refuge in Mexico, tens of thousands have succeeded in reaching the United States. There their legal status is normally extremely precarious, besides which they must survive in a culture and language vastly different from their own.

Carmen, a 42-year-old political exile who left her country six years ago for the United States, is divorced with three children. In Guatemala she worked as a teacher, coping with notoriously bad conditions. In the mid-1980s an estimated 800,000 schoolchildren were without classrooms, thousands of teachers were unemployed, illiteracy rates were high and general educational standards very low. Between 1981 and 1984, a reported 235 teachers were killed or disappeared in Guatemala, and Carmen fled the country in fear of her life. In the United States she works for a Guatemalan solidarity organisation and is involved in the women's movement.

I left Guatemala because what we call the official death squads came to my house looking for me. When I heard about it I left home immediately. I started living in different places, running from my own shadow, I was so afraid. In those days the police and the army stopped people often, and I was always afraid of being recognised, because I didn't know whether they were carrying my picture or not. You read and hear so much about the persecution of other people that when it's your turn you imagine the worst. It's as if they're looking for *you* with a picture of *you*.

I didn't want to leave my country so I went into hiding. I was always afraid and it was making my family ill, because they wouldn't hear from me for days. I have two sons, teenagers now. They stayed with my parents when I went into hiding but they stopped going to school. I was afraid for them because there are so many cases of death squads kidnapping children when they can't get the parents. Nevertheless, I managed to maintain some contact with them. When

I was in the city, I would let my neighbours know that I was around so that they could pass on the word and my parents would bring my children to see me. But I didn't do that often: most of the time I was too scared — for them as well as myself.

Being in hiding was very difficult: I thought I was going crazy. There were many nights when I couldn't sleep or, if I did, I had nightmares of being surrounded and tortured. One of the things that I feared most was sexual abuse. You hear that that is what they do to women whom they capture. My fear must have been quite visible because one day, when I went to rent a room, the landlady said to me, 'What's wrong? You seem afraid.' I told her that I was sick and that I needed to rest. She told me that if I wanted to live there we would have to trust each other. 'If you're running away from the police or if you killed someone, feel free to tell me,' she said. Still I couldn't tell her. I was too scared and I couldn't trust anyone. She also suspected that I might be a prostitute, though she didn't say so directly, and she obviously didn't want that sort of thing in her house. She was actually very kind. I remember one night I was so terrified that I couldn't control myself and I started to scream. She gave me a tranquilliser and offered to let me sleep in her room, but I didn't trust her. Even with the tranquilliser, I still couldn't sleep until morning. That was usually what happened — I would wait for dawn before I would sleep. It seems that during the day you are not so frightened. This kind of fear is partly cultural. Here in the United States children and teenagers are so independent of their parents, but we Latin Americans are not. We are always surrounded by our families and when we have to be by ourselves it is very, very difficult. At home, I always slept with my sisters and my family was always around. Suddenly there I was a grown-up woman, and I was afraid to be by myself — even though I'd been divorced for quite a while and had had to raise my kids practically alone.

My family put a lot of pressure on me to leave Guatemala and go to the United States. I wanted to go to Mexico because it's so close to Guatemala and I thought that maybe we could arrange to see each other on the border. But my parents said that Mexico wasn't safe and that if I didn't go to the United States they wouldn't send me the children, because they were concerned about what might happen to them.

Exile in the United States

I arrived in the States in 1983 and stayed with a friend who was already living here. The first thing you do, of course, is look for a job as a live-in maid, which keeps you off the streets and allows you to save money. You don't have to worry about an apartment and bills, and I wanted to save a lot so I could bring my children over as soon as possible. I had been a teacher in Guatemala, but I felt that I could worry about my career later on.

You can get a job as a maid very easily. The hard part is being shut up inside a house all day long for five or six days a week, with no chance of going anywhere. You have to think about housework all the time, so it's only good at night when you're asleep. I was always counting the weeks, and calculating how much money I could save. I knew that my boys were OK, but I wanted them with me because I was afraid that something might happen to them.

It seems that life is not fair. Most of the things that men and women face affect women more. It's not so hard for a man to leave his children as it is for a woman, as we are more attached to them. Also, women are always afraid of being attacked or sexually abused. At one time I was cleaning houses during the day and working in a factory in the evenings, where I would finish about 12:30 at night. I was afraid of being attacked as I lived in a very dangerous street. So whenever I arrived at my street and saw that there were men around, I would go to the 7-11 [24-hour supermarket] and ask the people there to keep an eye on me, because I was going to sleep in my car in the parking lot. They understood because they knew that the street was very dangerous. I often didn't sleep much, just staying in the car and waiting for a safe moment to go home to bed. It was awful, because the next day I had to get up very early to clean the house.

It seems that in recent years my life has been dominated by fear. In Guatemala, it was political fear. I don't remember ever being afraid of other people there. I had three sisters and sometimes we would go out together to a party nearby and would happily walk on the streets at night. However, the fear of being 'disappeared' or killed weakened my nerves, so that when I came here I wasn't the same woman. I'm still not the person I was before. I'm not completely together. I can't handle the fear, I cannot control it the way I used to. I guess it's partly because I don't have my family here, and if something happened to me, then what would happen to my children? Who would take care of them?

Personal change

Since I've been in the United States I have learned a lot, not only about Guatemala but also about other parts of the world. You don't have the chance to in Guatemala. Being aware of what is going on makes you change, you cannot live life in the same way. You cannot have personal goals like 'I want to be rich', 'I want to have my own house', or 'I want to have a house to leave my children'. I used to have those dreams, but I've changed. No matter what you do, your children will have their own problems and they will resolve them themselves. You should put your own energy elsewhere.

Here in the United States I have succeeded in being able to communicate with women. In Guatemala, I couldn't because it was boring for me to talk to women. Chatting about the house, the children, the husband, what you're going to cook for dinner, the holidays ... I found it boring. There were so many other things to be concerned about! So I could only communicate with men because they were involved; women weren't. It was sad.

Here, though, I find it so easy to communicate with women. It didn't happen right away — it's been gradual. At first, I waited to see how women felt here, and as they talked it began to show. I find it easy now. Sisterhood is a great feeling — I feel it deep inside and it's great! For many years, I didn't feel that sense of togetherness. We are sisters because we are trying to change things, we are defending our rights. Now I see the potential of a best friend in every woman. I don't see a competitor, I don't see someone who is going to say 'You're a dreamer, a loser'. Instead there is a challenge: 'OK, you are wrong about this, but let's discuss it'. That's what I've found here, and it's really good.

The situation in Latin America is so different from that in the United States, although there are people living in terrible conditions here as well, and there is discrimination. I think that each country's social, political and cultural reality sets the context for women's struggle, the way it develops and the way it is expressed. Problems are similar in the US and Latin America, but they take a different form, so reactions are different.

I'd love to go back to Guatemala if I could, if it was safe for me and if I wouldn't feel afraid — in an ideal world, in other words. I think I would have difficulty figuring out how to organise women, which is the only way to create awareness. I would be arguing with both men and women all the time. You know, 'Why are you letting your husband do that to you?' or, 'Why are you doing that? Don't you have any self-respect?' ... But who knows? So many things have happened in Guatemala that I might not need to struggle that much. Women may well have changed a lot — people change, you know.

'Don't talk...'

A *ladina* researcher in her 50s talks about the fear pervading life during the dictatorship of General Jorge Ubico (1931-1944).

From time to time, when we were a little better-off, my parents would employ someone to stay in the house and look after my grandmother because my mother was disabled by illness. The house would fill with despair then, because we couldn't talk openly. Someone was always telling you to keep quiet. It was the same when the postman came. 'Be careful, don't talk to the postman', or 'Don't say anything to the people who come to sell potatoes.'

The corner shop was the worst place. 'Don't ever mention anything that goes on in this house', we children were told. There were definite rules about talking — you were supposed to say absolutely nothing to strangers. That was the biggest worry of all.

Life as a Carib student leader

A steamy port on the Caribbean coast and a town on the lush banks of the Rio Dulce with the improbable name of Livingston are the principal habitat of one of Guatemala's smallest ethnic groups: the Garifunas or black Caribs. Unless visitors make a special trip to the Caribbean coast they will probably be unaware of the existence of this community, which still holds to its customs.

Little ever appears in the national press about Caribs and they hold no national government posts. They scarcely participate in the political life of the country outside their own area, which to a large degree escaped the brunt of the political violence of the 1980s. They have not, however, escaped the social problems that are rife in Guatemala: extreme poverty, a lack of basic services and racial discrimination.

Elizabeth, a young Carib leader in the student movement at the National University of San Carlos is a dynamic activist who has received death threats from paramilitary death squads. These threats cannot easily be ignored, considering that 11 leaders of the University Student Association have disappeared, including seven leaders who were abducted in 1989 and hundreds of other students and university workers have 'disappeared' in recent years.

The area around Puerto Barrios is very different from other parts of Guatemala. We have a different culture, the Garifuna culture. The founders were Garifunas from the Caribbean coast. I am the product of a mixture of cultures: the Garifunas intermarried with the native inhabitants and another ethnic group, the Araguaco Carib, was born. I think of myself as an Araguaco Carib.

The Caribs are rather isolated from the rest of the country. We are a coastal people. Few of us have the chance to improve ourselves and get an education.

Women in this part of the country are very restricted. We are relegated to the purely domestic sphere. There's a lot of *machismo*. Women are considered the 'weaker sex' and unable to participate

102

in fields such as politics. Even women who have been educated are always considered inferior to men. We do not have access to broad participation in local society. Few women have occupied positions of any authority. Today, for the first time in the history of the Puerto Barrios area, we have a woman governor, who got the post through her political party, the Christian Democrats. So far, however, she has not taken part in the decision-making. There is always someone behind her giving the orders.

There is a lack of solidarity between men and women in this part of the country. We have a lot of prostitution and single mothers. A man can have up to three women. Prostitution is common in port cities, and for many single mothers the easiest way out is to sell their bodies. It's a social problem: the conditions that exist here encourage it.

I come from a poor family. My father worked on the docks in Puerto Barrios and died when I was two years old. My mother is a seller. She brought us up on her own — it's been hard for her because we are a large family, with seven children. I'm the only one of my family who has managed to get to university. I am very privileged, because within my ethnic group very few women or men have access even to secondary education. It was a big effort for me to get here.

In the more traditional families, there are many restrictions on women entering university. Mothers believe that you go away to study, you graduate, then you get married and that's the end of it. My mother is different. She has had to struggle a lot and she believes that women have a great deal to contribute. She supported my coming here, and awakened in me the desire to survive, come what may. But her position was clear: she would support my secondary education and then it was up to me. In fact, the first thing I had to do when I arrived in the city was to get a job, because I had to pay the rent.

When I came to the university there was an additional pressure. In the capital, women from the coast are seen as being different. Men think we are 'easy'. They vulgarly refer to us as being 'hot' and they try to use us. There were only women students in the School of Social Work, which is a 'women only' career in Guatemala. Supposedly, only effeminate men study social work. I don't agree with this distinction because the first social workers were men. But it meant that I became aware that I was seen as 'easy' only when I began to have contact with students from other faculties. My first reaction was to become aggressive. I thought 'Who do they think they are?' I didn't understand it. But, little by little, I found a place for myself and since I joined the University Student Association (AEU) I've had a taste for protesting.

Fighting for a better way of life

Now I am the Training Secretary of a student organisation in the economics faculty. I am the only woman to hold a post on the executive board of the organisation. My task is to orientate new members, and to plan seminars discussing our goals and various topics such as the mass organisations. We keep a careful eye on human rights. The organisation has played an important role in the university, and many *compañeros* have had to go into exile. Many more have 'disappeared'. We have been on the receiving end of every type of intimidation from both the paramilitary death squads and groups within the university that are linked to the government.

As a woman, it is important for me to be in this post, and I think that I have conquered this space for other women. Next year they will be able to participate within a much broader spectrum, confronting the problems of *machismo* from the inside. There are no women's organisations in the university and there's a lack of women leaders. My interests are broader — although, at the professional level, one of my aims is to work with women's groups in order to promote the organisation of women in the rural areas.

When we talk of change, we are talking about the 'new man' and the 'new woman'. Many things can be changed but some things are very deeply rooted, as is *machismo* in Latin America. Structural change might take place, but it wouldn't necessarily affect *machismo*. This is where women have an enormous fight. In addition to participating in the struggle for national liberation, we have to carry on the struggle for our own demands. Both should go hand in hand, but the problem is that our struggle takes longer because the fight for women's liberation, in addition to being part of the struggle for liberation of all human beings, has its own specific demands. Discrimination against women exists in my organisation. Still, I think that we women have not won political space because we have yet not fought for it.

Apart from reflecting on the place that women occupy in society in general, the student movement's demands are linked to social demands. We are fighting for a true democracy, for freedom, for access to a better way of life and, fundamentally, for respect for human rights.

At the moment the student movement is going through a very critical period, and we have had a series of threats. I have received some of them. They come from paramilitary groups, like 'Jaguar Justice' who are capable of anything, and who have been following some of our members, abducting them in cars, threatening our families and making anonymous telephone calls. They say they are going to 'liquidate' us.

If this had happened last year I think I would have been afraid, but nowadays I am more sure of what I want and I don't worry. What would make me furious is if they killed me without my having done more. I think I have a lot to contribute.

Option for the poor

The vast majority of Guatemalans are Roman Catholic. When they talk about 'the church' they are referring to the Catholic Church, whose arrival with the Spanish conquest suppressed the native Mayan religion and whose hierarchy, until recently, has tended to collaborate, or comfortably co-exist, with Guatemala's ruling regimes. Within this church, however, is a growing sector that works for 'the preferential option for the poor'. This important element in Latin American liberation theology has played a key role in making Guatemala's poor aware of their social and economic conditions. It has also encouraged the growth of organisations attempting to bring about social change.

Hand in hand with this 'option for the poor' there is often a desire to change much of the church's structure and liturgy, the role of lay people, life in the religious orders and more. Clemencia, a *ladina* nun in her 30s, is actively involved in trying to bring about this kind of change. She takes considerable risks in her work (many priests and catechists have been assassinated in Guatemala and scores of nuns have been forced to leave), but she was most concerned during this interview that her identity be concealed from the Catholic Church hierarchy, with whom she has had many confrontations.

When I first entered the convent I was driven by a force that I didn't fully understand — I wanted to evangelise. I was motivated by the word of God and I wanted to talk to others about the Bible. It had been read a great deal to us as little ones at home and I thought it was important that children should know the Bible.

Since then, after much reflection and studying, I've realised that the religious life is a whole process. It has permitted me to dedicate my life to serving the people, and, above all, the most needy. In my congregation we work with other social classes, but I consider it a gift from God that I've always been able to work in Indian areas or in Guatemala City among the poor.

Naturally, I have thought about marriage and having children. Motherhood and the need to share your life with a man is a very big pull for a woman. But I have always dreamt of a new, structurally different religious life and have spent a lot of time trying to bring about this change. I have concentrated my energies on the struggle. Marriage and children would have restricted me. I wouldn't be so free to go from one place to another, often putting my life at risk.

The people with whom I work have helped me enormously to centre myself. Constantly giving, and being concerned for other people, has helped me to mature, to have affectionate relationships and to grow. I am a very emotional person, and I think this has helped me to be compassionate and to dedicate myself to my work with enthusiasm. This doesn't mean that I have never had emotional problems ... I fell in love once and I thought very deeply about what I wanted out of life. It was because of this force I felt within myself that I decided against love with this man. This is what my vocation is — a force that drives me. It was a difficult time, but I have no doubt that I made the right decision. I feel at home in the religious life and I'm sure that it is where I should be.

My other main problems have been in connection with other members of the community. In conflictive situations we have interpreted things differently. It is logical that we don't all view things in the same way, and this causes problems in a religious community. It is the feeling that I am in the right place that has helped me to understand all this as a normal process.

The church and human rights
I believe that the role of the church in Guatemala is first and foremost to evangelise. This evangelisation must be linked to concrete reality — not just quoting the gospel, but rather converting it into 'good news' for people. To me, this means supporting the poor, accompanying them and defending them from human rights violations, for example, which have not improved since there's been a civilian government here. Only the methods have changed. Maybe there aren't the same massacres, but there is still a lot of repression.

People talk about a democratic opening, but for how long? Trade union leaders and leaders of human rights organisations are coming out into the open now, but they are on lists and under very strict surveillance. People are afraid, exceedingly afraid. Few dare speak freely. It is still very difficult to find people willing to be group leaders and to speak out. The repression continues in a different form.

I think that the church has been a bit behind in dealing with this. This is understandable, however, because we have experienced considerable repression. Many catechists and some 20 priests have been murdered. This has caused a great deal of fear and apprehension within the church, especially within the church hierarchy: a fear of accompanying and supporting a suffering people, of defending the cause of the poor. The church has been constrained by fear and prudence that prevent it from defending human rights as it should.

I believe that the church should focus its work on areas where the poor are in the majority. It does in a sense, but this has been mainly through providing aid. There is nothing wrong with helping people, but the church should also be a liberating presence. Ordinary people should be allowed to speak, it shouldn't only be the priest who runs things. Lay people should be trained so that they have a say in the church.

Faith and indigenous cultures

The church should also make a priority of what you might call 'the evangelisation of culture' or 'the acculturation of faith'. The way that Indians are discriminated against really upsets me. I grew up in an area of the country which is almost totally indigenous, and when I was a child I thought of Indians as being dirty and strange. I never ever had an Indian friend. My father was a small landowner and the Indians would come to our house to consult us — to find out what to give a child when it was ill or something like that. It was as if we were superior beings. My opinions changed when I entered the religious life and began a process of reflection. It had never occurred to me before that Indians had dignity, that we were equal. Now that I have had a chance to study Indian cultures and have discovered their values and how rich they are, I think the church must change many of its attitudes. It must adapt to the people, not the people to the church. It must return to the cultural values and traditions of these people and incorporate them into the liturgy. There will have to be a new, revised liturgy — a return to the Mayan rites. I believe that these rites are the indigenous religious expression. The people have been told that they are pagan, but this is only so when viewed from the Western perspective. The Indians understand their rites as communicating with God. The church must recognise this and incorporate them into the liturgy. Unfortunately, there are very few Indian priests, and fewer still who think in this way, and it is they who should take this up. I know of two who are making a big effort to acculturise faith — with some success because the Indians in their parishes now sing and express themselves in their own language. Why should Indians sing *ladino* hymns that have come from Spain?

Most importantly, Indians should speak out and take part in the liturgy. The symbols must change — the bread, for example. What does bread mean to Indians? Corn is the basis of their diet. The body of Christ for them is best expressed through the *tortilla*. And then there is the wine. For us Latin Americans, wine is not something you drink with meals. You drink it to get drunk, so it doesn't have the same connotation for us as it has for Europeans.

The church must help human beings as a whole, but it should give more priority to helping women escape their ignorance. I don't agree with those in the religious community who condemn women for using contraception. Really it should be up to the couple — they should decide which method, artificial or natural, they want to use, and they should be informed about all the methods available so they can decide which one is best for them. I don't believe that it is the church's role to tell them which method to use.

In Guatemala all poor people are suffering due to a generalised discrimination, disrespect and contempt. I am hoping for social change that will cater for at least the basic needs of the poor, and I believe that this will bring about justice and peace.

First woman Labour Minister

Paradoxically, it was in Guatemala, one of the least developed countries in Latin America, that a woman was first appointed to a government post as important as that of Minister of Labour. In fact, Catalina, a 43-year-old *ladina*, is the only woman on the entire American continent ever to have held this post. A powerful political figure in the ruling Christian Democrat Party, Catalina identifies with its progressive wing. She was Minister of Labour in the Christian Democrat government which took office in January 1986. During her period as Labour Minister, Catalina attempted to promote interest in women's conditions by expanding the work of the National Women's Office (Onam).

In June 1987, at the time of this interview, Catalina was still Labour Minister, a post she resigned from shortly afterwards. In January 1991 she became president of the National Congress.

I became involved in politics because my mother had a very strong Christian commitment to community work. I used to accompany her on her charitable activities, and I became interested in the concerns of the poorest. I wanted to study sociology when I finished school, but there were no sociology courses in Guatemala, and because I was a woman my parents didn't want me to study at the national university. They said that no woman with any self-respect would go to the university because it was too risky. It was only because there was a Catholic university where some of the lecturers were priests whom my mother had worked with, that I got to go to university. I studied law, which was the nearest thing to what I was interested in.

I quickly became interested in university politics, participating in the *Bufete Popular*, which gave legal advice to people of limited means. Then in 1970 some Christian Democrats invited me to join their party.

At the beginning I had problems because I was a woman. The party was very open to the participation of women, but we were not welcomed in political decision-making posts. Earlier on there had been women on the national directorate, but for a period of ten or twelve years there were no women in the leadership. So when I came to occupy a political post in the party there were some obstacles.

The 1970s was a very difficult time for the party. There was a lot of violence because our thinking was not considered 'democratic' and we were accused of being pro-communist. I was personally affected and had to leave the country for a while. One of my brothers was assassinated and two of my nephews 'disappeared'; we never saw them again. But fear never made me want to abandon politics, even though there was an attempt on my life when I was legal advisor to the National Workers' Congress (CNT). I've never, ever thought that this meant I should stop doing what I believe in.

Leadership will give women power

When I was first appointed Minister of Labour the trade unionists claimed that I had been given this post because I was a woman. They alleged that it was a form of psychological pressure against them — that they would be inhibited in the presence of a woman and would not be able to express themselves freely. That was how they used to feel. Nowadays, they often prefer to talk directly to me and when I'm away they wait for me to get back. They say that because I am a woman, I am more understanding, more moderate and more conciliatory....

The fundamental problem for women in Guatemala is that it is difficult for us to fulfil ourselves. We fulfil ourselves through others — through our husbands, our children, through an 'other'. We are always working for others; there is seldom a moment when others are working for us. Our satisfactions are always indirect.

I believe that the only way this can be overcome is by doing the things that we supposedly shouldn't do. Any woman, regardless of her situation, only needs incentives. I've seen this particularly with *campesina* women. They only need a little push at the beginning, then they can go ahead and fulfil themselves. The important thing is that they become conscious and confident enough to do something. In Guatemala, there are women in cooperatives, in Indian *cofradías* [primarily male religious societies linked to a cult of a saint], in religious groups, and women are very much present in political parties. It is not that women don't participate, it is just that they lack access to positions of leadership and direction. I believe that in many cases this is due to self-limitation. Women are not aware of their enormous potential. They reach mid-level positions with enthusiasm, but becoming the head of something, 'the boss', that's where the problems begin.

Nevertheless, to get into leadership positions, it is crucial that women participate. The type of organisation in which they participate is not so important, what matters is that they participate — that they don't work in isolation or only with informal groups, because these don't generate power.

This is what has happened to feminism in Guatemala; it has no formal organisation, no organised pressure groups. Women stand more chance of achieving leadership positions, better working conditions and better treatment at all levels, if they participate in organisations of a more social nature. But in Guatemala feminists have not done this because they only want to organise women to become feminists....

Up until 1983, there was no women's organisation in my party. Then one was formed to provide women with training and education useful for different areas of the party. The women don't stay exclusively in the women's organisation. If women form a block within a political party, the resulting isolation makes them a 'ghetto' within the party.

I don't know if it's just my inclination, or political-professional bent, which makes me think that it is so important to have women in leadership roles. The truth is that power relations exist everywhere, not just in political parties. People usually associate politics with parties, but politics is everything that is related to power, decision-making and authority. Leadership will give women power.

Censorship

A 50-year-old *ladina* woman talks about being a journalist in times of repression.

Many journalists have been assassinated in Guatemala — women included. Irma Flaguer, for example. She was very committed, very brave, and very frank, particularly in her writing. She was assassinated in 1980. This sort of thing rather restricts your personal fulfilment as a journalist...

Really, what we journalists did was censor ourselves. There was never any 'official' censorship. The government or groups with an interest in such-and-such a thing not being published did not intervene directly with the newspapers. If you published something that a certain sector didn't like, they didn't criticise you for writing it, nor were you taken to court for libel. Their criticism arrived in the form of bullets, or being 'disappeared'.

So there was overwhelming self-censorship. We knew the reality of the situation we were living under. Of course, sometimes what was taking place was so obvious that you couldn't censor yourself, and then anything could happen...

Faith in the far-right

Right-wing politicians in Guatemala tend to vacillate within a multitude of ultra-right parties of various hues that change their identity with virtually every election. The convoluted names and logos of these transitory political groupings make only ephemeral appearances on the nation's electoral ballots. In contrast, the leaderships of these parties seem to go on for ever, as the same names appear at the head of each new grouping. Yet while the parties might change, the politics usually remain the same. Basically, all right-wing parties (which in Guatemalan politics usually signifies ultra-right) are anti-communist, anti-trade union, authoritarian and dedicated to protecting the interests of a privileged few. Their antiquated 'red under every bed' philosophy and siege-like mentality might seem quaint were it not for their having led, both directly and indirectly, to the deaths of many Guatemalans branded as 'subversives' and 'communists' for trying to improve basic living conditions in their country.

There are few women in leadership positions in such parties, although their particularly strident politics are made use of in speeches at political rallies. An exception is Marta, a 49-year-old *ladina* and great-niece of the much feared dictator, General Jorge Ubico, who ruled Guatemala for 13 years until 1944. Although she is no longer assistant general secretary of the Guatemalan National Action Party, she is still an important party ideologue.

My family was well-to-do. My great-grandfather owned some properties, so we had enough money to 'get by'. We weren't multi-millionaires, but we had enough. My great-uncle was President Jorge Ubico. He didn't have any children and my father was his only nephew, so the relationship was very close. President Ubico was very much the conservative type, very upright, very paternalistic, very honest and very protective towards Indians. I think that his was the last honest government in Guatemala. He resigned in 1944, leaving General Ponce in power. That October there was a revolution to overthrow General Ponce. When it happened we were living in a house in the town centre. It was six o'clock in the morning and someone said there was a tank on the corner pointed towards the house. I was very scared. People from the new government came and searched our house. I don't know what they were looking for. My parents took me to hide me in my maternal grandfather's house because of the danger. Of course, we were very much on the wrong side at the time. From early on, I've been very exposed to politics.

I've been a practising lawyer for 15 years. As my children are now grown up and I've been divorced for 12 years, I feel free to involve myself in risky situations, such as politics.

My children are very supportive towards me. We have an excellent relationship, very friendly. A few years ago I was thinking of leaving Guatemala because I was afraid of a totalitarian government taking over. That, and my sense of frustration from constantly having to work with people of a very low educational level. Being a lawyer puts me in touch with the government bureaucracy, which is awful. So we considered leaving. But my children said, 'No, we want the right to live in our own country. So, if you think you can do anything about the situation go ahead, and we'll support you.'

The Guatemalan Nationalist Party

I am a founding member of the Guatemalan National Action Party. It's a fairly new party — we've been working for a year and a half with different groups of people. People are looking forward to having a conservative group that they can believe in. They have lost faith in most of the traditional conservative parties because, in many ways, they haven't acted in a very civilised manner.

We are trying to unite all the centre-right parties. We are not having much success with the leadership, but we have had a lot of influence among people at the lower levels, especially in the CAN (Authentic Nationalist Central), which is one of the groups further to the right than I tend to enjoy. We have also had people come from the MLN (National Liberation Movement). In terms of our philosophy, we believe in Western values. We are very much against Marxism because we have experienced it first-hand, and we know what it is about — take the government that we had in 1952, which thank heavens we got rid of [democratically elected President Jacobo Arbenz was overthrown in a CIA-sponsored coup in June 1954].

Central America seems to be in increasing danger of invasion by totalitarian groups. Communism is currently the worst threat, and we definitely don't want that for our countries. We believe in freedom, and we have seen that it is the poor who suffer most from totalitarianism, especially Marxism.

So far, our party's limited funds have come in the form of donations from the rich, people who are very conscious of the need to create a new movement to prevent a future communist system. They have confidence in us mainly because of the people who head the party and our ideas. We are trying to get international support, and I think that we can make this movement grow a great deal. Our party believes in a civilian government, but with a place for the army, since we are under a constant threat. We feel that we should have a strong, professional army dedicated to protecting the territory and the population from foreign invasion, and to supporting the Constitution and whoever is legally and freely elected. There is still a threat of communism here, and it's not true that the army has pacified the country. There are still guerrilla groups in at least eight departments. They strike and then they quieten down for a while. At this point, the army can control problems inside Guatemala. But we can't forget El Salvador — if it were to fall into the hands of totalitarian Marxists, the Salvadoran guerrilla would simply come across the border and start messing around in Guatemala.

My party also feels that we need to stimulate and provide security for local and foreign investment. We would propose freezing taxes for at least five years. If we gave investors the security of knowing that they can get their money out of the country (after paying any taxes that they should pay under Guatemalan law), it would stimulate both foreign and local investment. People like to be sure that their money is safe, that nobody will take it away.

It is also important to have enough authority and popular support to control crime. Everywhere you go in Guatemala people's main protest is, 'We are so insecure! We are being assaulted all the time! We are being robbed.' If you go into the city centre your car is likely to be stolen. It never used to be this bad in Guatemala. And crime affects the lower classes more, because they live in areas that are vulnerable to attack.

On the party's attitude to abortion — basically, we wouldn't be enthusiastic. It's not a very good, responsible or legitimate way out.

It would also be too difficult and dangerous to legalise it here. Personally, I think that if we legalised abortion in Guatemala, the situation would just become much worse than it is. People are not educated enough to be responsible. But I do think that something should be done to make men more responsible for their children. At the moment, they can get away with anything.

On the question of the indigenous population, something that should have been done a long time ago is to provide bi-lingual education during the first three years of schooling so that Indian children can start learning Spanish. This is the only way for them to communicate and gradually increase their knowledge. As long as they don't speak Spanish, how are we to get our message across or give them information about anything? Even political parties run into this problem — we have to find interpreters to convey messages in the 22 different languages. The make-up of this country is really absurd. I can understand why it is so difficult for Europeans to comprehend what is happening here.

With sufficient education Indians will probably gradually abandon their customs and their language. If it were possible for them still to speak their own language as well as Spanish, then fine. But the natural tendency would be for it to disappear. To tell you the truth, I've always felt that it is very cruel to assume that Indians should keep to their local customs. We have to catch up with the times, with the 20th century. I wouldn't want to impose anything on anyone, but I think that they would want to be educated if they realised that they could trade more profitably if they were familiar with numbers and knew how to do business in Spanish. They are bound to want to. They are not stupid or different from the rest of us. There are very bright people among them. They just don't have opportunities...

You can imagine that if they still have trouble accepting women active in politics in developed countries like Britain and the United States, it is much more extreme in Guatemala. Every time I go on trips to the smaller towns, people look at me trying to figure out who I am married to, whose secretary I am, or even whose lover I am! It's very funny when they finally realise that I am active, that I do have an opinion, and that I am participating in politics because I have ideas for change in Guatemala and other countries in Central America.

Revolution and love in the URNG

For three years, from 1979 until 1982, Irma fought in one of the armed organisations that now make up the Guatemalan guerrilla front known as the Guatemalan National Revolutionary Unity (URNG). She now lives in exile in another Latin American country and is involved in political work on Guatemala. She is part of a group of former combatants who are attempting to re-evaluate their role in the Guatemalan political process, as well as to analyse the setbacks suffered by the guerrillas in the mid-1980s.

A young *ladina*, Irma is working toward developing consciousness on women's issues among those involved in the revolutionary struggle in Guatemala.

I had to leave Guatemala because I was in the guerrilla and the army was looking for me. They considered the military unit I was in to be 'public enemy number one'. In fact, this unit was very hard hit. I am the only one that survived out of my squad. The repression was so bad we didn't sleep at night and every dawn we thanked God we were still alive. When we were out in the street we were terrified that we would be caught. As soon as we got home we would feel relieved. But we would quickly feel afraid again, thinking that we would be attacked while we were in the house. This insecurity made it impossible to remain in Guatemala.

When you join a revolutionary organisation you discover that normality is abnormality and, little by little, you grow accustomed to abnormality and instability. It's not that you say to yourself, 'I'm going to have to leave my partner, my children, or my family if necessary' ... You get involved without being fully aware of all the implications. Gradually you get used to all this, and if the moment arises when you have to leave your family, then you do so. It's because you have revolutionary tasks and they determine what you do. You don't have a lot of time to reflect on it. At least, that was how it used to be.

I believe that today we revolutionaries should think about these things, because they have limited the participation of many women and men who want to get involved in the revolutionary struggle, but who don't want to be tied by the condition that they must break with their families or lead an abnormal life. It's a question of security... Most important to me was my life. If you know that the army could kill or kidnap you, then you opt for leaving your family rather than causing them problems too.

I remember I went to see my family around the time they kidnapped one of my husband's brothers. My mother told me not to come home any more because the army had taken him past our house and she was terrified. It was then a long time since I had lived with my family, due to security problems. I had got married, not out of a belief in marriage, but rather as part of the facade of normality that we had to present to other people. My husband was known publicly and we had information that the army was looking for him. It was thought that being married would make it less problematical for him. On the contrary, it made it more problematical for me...

We lived in a safe house, a house belonging to the organisation. We lived with another *compañera* and we all shared the housework between us. I think my husband was one of the most exemplary people in the revolutionary organisation because he did his share of the housework in addition to working hard at his other tasks. For example, we lived in an area where we only had water one day a week, so we washed all the clothes on this day. I have a little girl and there were always nappies to wash. So the two of us, he and I, just got to it with a big mound of clothes and started washing.

I was only 19 when I got married, and to me this was my 'big love'. It turned out that it wasn't so big, because after we had been together for a year, I felt that I didn't love him any more. To me he had been the ideal revolutionary, but after living with him as a man... I was restless; I wanted to know more about the world. Participation in the revolutionary organisations opens up all sorts of new areas for women. I separated from my husband quite a while before I went into exile.

Being a *guerrillera*

At first I was doing political work in the organisation. Then I got involved in military action after the army had launched a major offensive in which many of my closest *compañeros* were killed. Part of my eagerness to get involved in military work was because I felt that the army must not be allowed to act with such impunity. Military action seemed to be the area where I could best put into practice the hatred I felt for the army.

I like military work a lot. Something that gives me a lot of secret satisfaction is being a woman and being familiar with military tactics. Nevertheless, I saw many instances where women were under-estimated, and I fought against this. In one training session, for example, the *compañero* instructing us was explaining a series of obstacles through which we had to pass. There were only two women, the rest were men. While he was explaining what we had to do, the other woman said to me, 'I'm not doing it, no way.' 'I am', I said, and got into line.

I was fifth in line; the other woman got in behind me. I started running and went through all the obstacles. Then came the most difficult. I stopped and started trembling when I saw where I had to jump to: it was really high. 'Jump', said the instructor. 'I'll jump', I said, but without my weapon.' 'No', he said, 'with your weapon — you're a *guerrillera*, aren't you?' 'Without my weapon', I insisted. But, in the end he forced me to jump and luckily I managed. Afterwards the other woman jumped, too. On our way back, the instructor said to me, 'I know I really pressured you into jumping, but I did it because the four men in front of you had refused to jump and after you did it then they had to do it.' It was a kind of stimulus for the men, to compete with a woman — a challenge to their honour and dignity.

At that time, there was only one woman on the National Directorate of the organisation, but there were many women at other levels. There were fewer women in the military units, maybe two to every 17 men. I think that sometimes women create obstacles for themselves, on top of those that men create, because there were no actual objections to women forming part of the military units. There was, however, a consensus that only women should be responsible for taking care of the children and providing the medical services. And if *compañeras* were mothers, then the task of looking after their children fell mainly on them and not on their *compañeros*. To a certain degree, the fathers were irresponsible towards their children. I think that this is partly because within the organisations, and the popular movement in general, there has never been a sector specifically concerned with women's issues. Instead, we women have been involved in the struggle against capitalism, the crisis and repression, without discovering our own demands. This has meant that these have not been dealt with by the organisation either.

Guatemala is such a polarised society, there are no half measures, and this oppressive condition is reflected in the revolutionary organisations, which are not democratic. Their method of struggle is guerrilla war and an army-type structure governs, so orders are given. It's not quite as crude as that, but normally you do what the command tells you to without questioning it.

The instability of couple relationships in the organisations is terrible. It's awful for the woman who does not accept being moved to a certain area of work because she thinks that her talent lies in some other aspect of the revolutionary struggle. This means that her *compañero* will be moved to another house, or another front. The woman will end up somewhere else, and the relationship nearly always breaks up. Women in the organisations do not get together to talk about these things; absolutely not. Within the organisations what is discussed is the fight for the new society in economic and social terms, but the women's problem is not dealt with specifically. I think that it is probably only now, amongst we *compañeras* in exile, that an uneasiness about this aspect of the movement is being voiced.

When people talked about feminism I used to scoff. I understood feminism to be about women who are antagonistic towards men. I also believed that when the revolution triumphed women would automatically be liberated as well. I don't believe that any more. Women will first have to embark upon an internal ideological struggle so that they can begin to remove the impediments that society has historically imposed on them, and then take up the struggle against patriarchy. Both can be done at the same time. They don't have to wait until they are really advanced in order to get involved. I don't agree with a feminism that is antagonistic to men, because I think it is obstructive. It will not solve women's problems. If economic conditions do not change, the objective conditions for women's liberation will not exist.

In principle, I agree with a Marxist feminism that holds that socialism creates the objective conditions for women's liberation. But the revolutionary process must be accompanied by a profound ideological struggle to change the mentality of both men and women in order to construct a new world and a new humanity.

Widows fight for dignity and unity

In September 1988 a group of young Guatemalan women, mainly Indian and widowed as a result of the civil war, held their first national assembly in Guatemala City. The women announced the formation of the National Co-ordinating Committee of Guatemalan Widows, known by its Spanish acronym as Conavigua.

Conavigua was the first public 'women only' organisation to emerge within Guatemala due to the current conflict, and it is virtually 100 per cent indigenous. Its overall objective is to fight for the 'dignity and unity of women'. Great emphasis is placed on women's, especially Indian women's, involvement in the social and political life of Guatemala. Its members' demands for themselves and for their children include: alleviation of their most immediate needs in the areas of food, medical care, housing and clothing; government assistance in meeting education costs; and legislation to protect the interests of widows and poor women. They also want to recover the remains of their dead husbands and to give them a Christian burial. Not surprisingly, Conavigua has run into problems with the Guatemalan army. The military fear the potential power of an organisation of this type in a country with an estimated 45,000 widows.

Manuela, a member of Conavigua's executive committee, is a *Cakchiquel* Indian woman in her early 30s with two young children. She considers herself a widow although she cannot be certain that her husband is dead. He 'disappeared' in 1985.

When I was seven years old I started work so that I'd be able to go to primary school. I earned five cents a day looking after little children. A school note book cost three cents at the time, so I was able to afford it. Then our parish priest noticed that I got on well with people and invited me to take part in the Christian courses he gave. I learned that God wants peace for his people, that He doesn't want you to think only of yourself, but to take into account the situation of others. I began to understand a lot of things.

When I was about 18 I was the leader of a youth group. After the earthquake, when many houses collapsed and many people died, we got together with lots of other groups. Little by little I became involved in organising co-operatives and Christian groups. One of these was a group seeking to build a local hospital to benefit the whole community. Whilst working on this project I obtained a scholarship to do a nursing course in Cobán. However, some people who were collaborating with the army didn't believe that I was leaving to study. They thought I had gone to join the *guerrilla*. This caused a lot of problems. In 1980 the army started looking for me and my situation became difficult. Still, with my parents' encouragement I carried on with my work. Then the army took over the village and built a military base. They started picking up a lot of the community leaders — catechists, co-operativists and youth group leaders. So I had to leave my village and go to the capital.

At the end of 1982, I heard that the army had gone to my home, and when they couldn't find me or my brothers and sisters they took my father away. He was 58 at the time, and involved only in church work. This upset me deeply because he'd never done anybody any wrong.

Eight days later, the army raided the house again and took away my sister. During the raid, the army officer told my mother not to worry about my father any more because he was 'at peace'. 'Be content', he said, 'he's not in pain any more. He didn't suffer much.'

Widowhood
I met my husband here in the city, through my work. He was also a leader, a *campesino* leader. We were in the same situation, we'd both had to leave our villages and come to the capital. I was very lonely at the time, I'd broken off all communication with my family, for their safety and mine. He was company for me, and I felt a little bit safer. At least the affection I no longer had from my family, I now felt with him. But we were only together for two years. I don't really know what happened to him. On 24 May 1985 he left for work and he never came back, so he is 'disappeared'. At the end of 1987, I was told he was being held at the Chimaltenango military base, but I was too afraid to do anything. I knew that it was the army that had taken him, but I was frightened because so many people have been abducted who never reappear. I can't really believe that he could

still be alive, although I still hope that he is and that one day he'll come back. But I know the reality of my country.

I have two children, one is five years old and the other is six. As they are still very small I've never properly explained to them about their father. The older boy knows. He was only two at the time, but he went everywhere with his father and he can't get it out of his mind: 'My daddy left me, all of a sudden he went away'. Through my conversations with other women he has come to realise that his father is 'disappeared'. I've told him that I don't know if he will come back or not. 'Who has got him? What happened?', he asks. I tell him that I simply don't know. Now the children fear that we won't be able to stay together. 'Daddy went away without telling us where', they say. 'He disappeared, so might you.' This is the lot of the woman whose husband is 'disappeared'. Thousands of us suffer in this way. Nevertheless, our suffering has helped us to understand our social situation and it encourages us to be more active in changing it. We know that if women don't do something, this killing is never going to end.

Learning to defend ourselves
I became involved in Conavigua when I was invited to attend one of its meetings. Like many women, as I became conscious of our situation I gradually lost my fear. The truth is that people are traumatised by all these disappearances, by so much suffering and waiting. It took me nearly two years to shake off my trauma and to see our other needs: poverty, unemployment, and lack of food for the children. So many widows have these problems.

Now I am working full time for Conavigua. As the organisation grows, a great deal of time and effort is required. Especially since only a few of us can read and write, so we have to contribute more.

More than 5,000 women belong to Conavigua. Virtually all of us are Indians and we suffer enormous discrimination. The Indian woman is usually the one who retains most vestiges of Mayan culture, evident in her clothing and in the way she speaks. Her Spanish is not so good and she cannot express herself well, so she is the one who suffers more.

Conavigua's biggest problem at the moment is that we don't have the funds for training, in literacy for example. One of our principal goals is for women to gain the skills necessary for us to be integrated into the social and political life of the country. For hundreds of years, Indian women have hardly participated at all because we have been dominated by men. A lack of education has also limited our integration into society. Because of poverty we have been brought up to work, rather than to go to school. As soon as we were able we had to learn how to weave, to clean the house, to take the animals to pasture and to look for work in the countryside. We have been very isolated within our communities. But now we want indigenous women to become part of society and to participate in its development.

There are ignorant and *macho* men in the villages who say that women have no right to get organised because we are only women. They look upon women solely as objects. When women start to get involved and go to meetings we have been able to defend ourselves against sexual abuse, and that's what a lot of men don't like. Many *compañeros*, however, are aware of the situation — mainly catechists and community leaders who are interested in the development of the community — and they support the work of Conavigua. They know that it is the most important vehicle of expression for indigenous women.

How we organise

Conavigua committees are formed at various levels: hamlet, village, town and department. There is no restriction on age. Everything depends on the women's willingness and desire to defend herself. Our main objective is to defend our rights and dignity, and also to achieve unity among women — especially among widows. Being organised is the only way women can demand our rights. It is the only way our voice can be heard. Nobody takes any notice of you on an individual basis.

Our meetings are generally for women only. Although, when we are in meetings with men — in union meetings, for example, where men are the majority — we don't feel inferior, or cheated. We always give our opinions wherever we can.

Many of our committees have been harassed by the army and women have had their lives threatened, because the military doesn't want us to be organised. Because we are widows, we are at the heart of this country's suffering. The army sees us as an enormous scar left behind by all the violence.

There are more than 45,000 widows in Guatemala and the military is afraid of what might happen if we were all to become organised.

From our point of view, they are the ones responsible for there being so many widows. Although big landowners are also to blame, because many Indian women's husbands became ill and died due to overwork on the *fincas*. Nonetheless, the vast majority of the women in Conavigua are widows as a result of the violence.

We are now beginning to communicate with a group of *ladina* women here in the city. We are aware that poverty affects them equally. It is the system that has divided us. We know that *ladina* women are also discriminated against, especially those in the squatter settlements, and we want to strengthen our contact with them. Indian women, however, are more vulnerable to discrimination. In the countryside the military have no respect for us. Not only are we subjected to sexual abuse, but we are also obliged to cook the soldiers' food and wash their clothes. There have also been a lot of rapes and many young girls and older women have become pregnant as a result. For widows, this has meant more children without a father. Some women have been raped by the same soldiers who killed their husbands! Because of their situation many of these women opted for abortion. A lot have had the children but then given them away...

This was most common between 1981 and 82, when women had to go to the military bases and work for the soldiers. Matters began to change when the first women's groups formed and women decided that there needed to be an organisation that would defend them — especially the widows, who were most subject to abuse since they didn't have husbands to protect them. It was only when the military started to force married women to work for them and their husbands objected, that the men of the community started to support the widows.

Organisation is the only way
Through Conavigua we hope that we women will learn to stand up for ourselves, to improve ourselves and to create a better future for our children. We don't want to leave them with the legacy of the past. Many children were witness to the massacres and saw the deaths of their fathers and mothers. Many lost both parents.

The least we hope to achieve is for women to realise that their participation is worthwhile. In Conavigua we have learned to care for each other and to understand our suffering. Before, women didn't talk about our suffering. We were closed up inside ourselves and our homes, and we didn't want to know about what had happened to anyone else. Now we have learnt to share our experiences and suffering, and as a result we have come to understand each other and our particular problem as widows better. For example, I talk to the other women in the organisation about feeling a need for affection. I feel this most when my children ask me where there daddy is and when he is coming back. It is not so much the need for a man, that's the least of it, but there are times when you feel lonely, when you need someone to talk to...

Although I have fears for my children because of my work, I feel that I have something to contribute to Conavigua and that children should learn about what their mothers go through. They also need to understand that organisation is the only way.